j133.1
T234
t

FEB 27 1981   CHEROKEE
Memphis and Shelby
County Public Library and
Information Center

For the Residents
of
Memphis and Shelby County

TRUE
GHOST
STORIES

TRUE GHOST STORIES

by Isabella Taves

Illustrated by Michael Deas

Franklin Watts
New York | London | 1978

**For Brian Maxey,
who knows a good monster when he sees one**

Library of Congress Cataloging in Publication Data

Taves, Isabella.
True ghost stories.

CONTENTS: My grandmother's ghost.—Ghostly—and ghastly—dogs.—Satan's kingdom.—The chocolate ghost. [etc.]
   1. Ghosts—Juvenile literature. [1. Ghosts]
I. Deas, Michael. II. Title.
BF1461.T38   131.1   78–2724
ISBN 0–531–02225–0

Text copyright © 1978 by Isabella Taves
Illustrations copyright © 1978 by Franklin Watts, Inc.
All rights reserved
Printed in the United States of America
5 4 3 2

CONTENTS

1. My Grandmother's Ghost   3

2. Ghostly—and Ghastly—Dogs   20

3. Satan's Kingdom   38

4. The Chocolate Ghost   61

5. Whiney the Monster   79

6. The Most Evil of All Creatures   96

CHEROKEE

MEMPHIS PUBLIC LIBRARY AND INFORMATION CENTER
SHELBY COUNTY LIBRARIES

TRUE GHOST STORIES

Chapter 1
MY GRAND-MOTHER'S GHOST

On winter evenings in Nebraska, when the wind howled and blew the snow in huge drifts outside our houses, my cousins and I would tumble into my Grandma Belle's little back room. There, snug in front of the fire, we would drink hot chocolate and eat her homemade sugar cookies. And she would tell us true ghost stories.

Our mothers didn't approve. They thought ghosts were a lot of superstitious nonsense. But Grandma Belle paid them no attention. For she knew better. From the time she was a child, she had listened to her mother tell true ghost stories she had heard as a child from her elders. She herself had seen ghosts. And she saw no reason why we, her grandchildren, shouldn't be prepared. Who knows, one of these days we might inherit her ability.

Our family were Scots Presbyterians who had come over from Scotland to America in a sailing vessel. My grandmother's mother, my great-grandmother Christie McIntosh, had been a girl of fourteen at the time. They had settled in a big old farmhouse in Canada, near friends who had come to the new country with them or before them. The farmhouse had a huge fireplace, so big even a tall man could walk into it. During the bitter winters, it was the only heat they had, so fires blazed constantly on the hearth. Food was cooked in big cast-iron pots that hung over the logs, and they baked bread in little ovens built into the brick walls of the fireplace.

After supper, the old folks used to gather in front of this fireplace. Their religion was very strict. They did not play cards or dance. And since there was no television or radio or movies, their only entertainment was telling stories. Not made-up stories, but stories of true experiences. And many of these were about people they knew who had seen ghosts or had visions of true events before they happened.

Most scientists don't believe in ghosts because they say that there is no scientific proof that there is life after death, or that these people who live in another world can communicate with us. But perhaps, in the days when my great-grandmother was a girl, people lived so simply and so close to nature that their minds weren't cluttered. They saw ghosts and visions that told them of the future.

At any rate, my great-grandmother believed in ghosts because she had heard her parents, and her aunts and uncles, tell of their experiences. Often, long after she was supposed to be in bed, she huddled in the shadows of the big country kitchen, listening to tales of ghosts and hauntings.

When she was eighteen, Christie McIntosh married a local boy, George Munro. He was a quiet boy, very ambitious and hardworking, who had come over from Scotland on the same boat as she had. He took his young bride to Le Mars, Iowa, because he had heard that it was wonderfully rich country for farming. It was, and he prospered. My great-grandmother Christie had nine children. Big families were the custom in those days, and the children had to make themselves useful helping out on the farm and in the house. Their amusements were few, so their mother used to entertain them by telling the ghost stories she'd heard as a child in Canada.

My grandmother was the second-born. Her older sister, poor little Jenny, died when she was six years old of diphtheria. When she was dying, her breathing was so harsh and dreadful they could hear her all over the big frame house. One night, when her mother was holding her, trying to ease her gasps for breath, Jenny's ghost appeared. It came through the window and stood in front of the sick child, stroking her hair and face. Jenny's mother was afraid, but the child wasn't. Suddenly, her breathing eased, and she looked up into her mother's face and smiled. A few minutes later she was dead.

Jenny's death made her younger sister, Belle, very sad. They had slept together in a big bed and Belle had loved Jenny very much. But her mother comforted her by saying, "Jenny's ghost looked just like Jenny when she was well. She was bright and happy, and I am sure Jenny is far happier

on the other side than she was here when she was so sick. She was glad to go."

Belle was red-headed and freckled, like her mother, and full of spunk. Belle used to say that if a ghost came for her, she would chase it away. Her brother Jim, when he got old enough, used to tease her by pretending he was a ghost, putting a pillowcase over his head and coming into the bedroom where she now slept alone. Sometimes he would be holding some chains he had smuggled in from the barn and he would shake them and moan. Instead of being scared, Belle would jump out of bed and chase Jim out of the room and up the stairs.

But one night Belle was given a glimpse into the world beyond this one.

It was July. Belle had just turned twelve and was feeling far too grown-up to join the younger children, who were in the back, playing hide-and-seek in the barn. Instead, she went outside and sat on the front steps. Iowa was a fine place for crops and the corn grew high. But the climate was not so good for human beings. Winters were very cold, with high winds blowing blizzard-strength across the plains, and summers were stifling hot on the prairies. Only after the sun went down did a refreshing breeze come across the parched lands.

She was enjoying the breeze and listening to her father and Jim talking about their team of horses. Jim was helping his father repair some harness.

Suddenly she saw a team of horses coming down the dirt road in front of the house. At this time of night, all the farmers nearby were home. Nobody came by unless there was an emergency. But even more peculiar, neither the horses nor the wagon they were pulling made any noise. The night was still, but the strange vehicle and even the animals seemed to be gliding above the ground.

As she watched, the horses turned up the lane leading to the farmhouse. The man holding the reins ran the feed store in Le Mars. Beside him sat the stationmaster at the railroad station and, of all people, the local barber who cut Papa's hair. But even odder was the sight of a coffin in the back of the wagon. Three more men were also in the back. She recognized Mr. Watts, who owned the furniture store, and his assistant, who sold the coffins they also carried. The third man was a stranger. But he, like the rest, was bundled up, as though it might be a winter night. And then she noticed something else. The wagon wasn't a wagon. It was a sleigh with runners. And the reason it was moving so silently was because it was floating above the ruts in the driveway.

She tried to call out. No sound came out of her mouth.

Then the worst thing of all happened. The men all got out of the sleigh. Still walking above the ground, they put the coffin on their shoulders, three men on each side, and headed toward where she was sitting. She jumped up. But the men with the coffin walked right through her. And as they were passing, she was submerged in a blast of the coldest air she had ever felt. Her teeth chattered. Her hands and feet turned to blocks of ice. She couldn't even catch her breath.

She ran into the house.

Her father looked at her in surprise. "What's wrong, Belle? You're shivering."

She was indeed. She thought she would never get warm again. But her brother Jim began to laugh. He thought Belle was trying to play a trick on them.

Belle rushed into her father's arms. "Look outside,

Papa. Some men have a coffin. I think they're ghosts. I recognized all but one. Maybe they're coming for me! Don't let them take me, Papa!"

Jim went to the door. "Nobody there, Papa. Belle is just trying to fool us. She's crazy."

Belle put her arms around her father's neck and clung to him, sobbing. "I'm not fooling. The men came in a sleigh and they had a coffin and, coming up the steps, they walked right through me."

Jim was having a wonderful time. He began running around the room, shouting, "Crazy Belle is going to die! Crazy Belle has seen her own ghostie!"

Papa held Belle tight, patting her head, ruffling her red curls. And her mother, hearing the commotion, came into the room from the kitchen.

She said sharply, "Jim, keep still. I have a headache. And, Belle, you ought to be ashamed of yourself, making up silly stories in this heat." Then she looked at her husband. "The idea of holding a big girl like Belle on your lap, like a little baby. Belle, go to your room. I'll be in shortly."

Belle obeyed. But she was recovered enough to give her brother a swat on the head as she passed him. That set him screaming.

Belle waited for her mother, sitting on the edge of the bed. The shivering started again, and she wrapped her bare arms around her thin body to keep warm.

When her mother finally came, the spanking she planned to give Belle was forgotten. She felt her daughter's cold hands and arms and then put a hand on her forehead. It was burning hot. She put Belle to bed with the usual home remedy, a wet, cold compress of many layers of flannel on her chest and several blankets. Then she brought her cups of hot tea with rock candy in it. The object was to break the fever.

Having her mother fuss over her made Belle feel better. Belle knew her mother loved her. But recently her mother had been tired and cross. Having so many children so close together had not been easy. And she was expecting another baby, her ninth. That, plus the heat, had made her cross and impatient.

So, although she was worried about Belle, she did not listen carefully when Belle told her what she had seen. And she did not take it seriously.

She just said, "Don't make up silly stories like that. I know you like to tease Jim. Sometimes I don't blame you, he gets on my nerves too. But please, this time, just forget it."

Belle tried. And Jim must have missed his sister, because when Belle was up and around again, out of bed, with the fever gone, he didn't tease her about seeing her ghosts. Soon everyone in the household had forgotten all about Belle's strange vision. Except Belle.

But before long, summer was over. Mamma's last baby was born, little Gilbreth. And it was time for school to begin. Belle and Jim and sister Hettie went back to school, taking with them George, Jr., who was just starting first lessons. After school, while Mamma took care of the new baby, Belle had charge of the three who were not yet in school but old enough to run around and get into mischief. She sometimes told them Mamma's ghost stories. But she never mentioned the men in the sleigh with the coffin. As time went on, she felt a little ashamed about it. What if it had been just her imagination?

Soon after Thanksgiving, Papa went to the auction in Omaha, Nebraska. He was going to buy some young horses and he promised Belle one of them would belong to her. She already rode bareback on the old farm horses, but this time he was going to buy her a saddle and reins.

While he was gone, the big snows started, and the days grew shorter. It was always more lonesome in the winter when Papa was gone. The children and their mother sat in the kitchen after supper, keeping warm by the big iron stove until it was time to go to bed. Now it was the younger children who used to beg for ghost stories. Belle and Jim pretended they were no longer interested. But as Belle listened, her own experience began to take on a new meaning. What if she really had seen something that might someday happen?

The idea scared her. She wanted to ask Mamma, but Mamma was always busy with the new baby these days. She decided to wait until Papa came home, which would be any day now.

A few nights later, when she was fast asleep, she was wakened by a hand on her arm. She sat up. The moon shining in the window was almost full, and with delight she saw her father's dear, kind face. He put his arms around her and held her tight, the way he had done when she was a little girl, just as he had the day she had seen the vision and was frightened. For a while, it was so good to have him there she didn't say a word. Then she started to ask him about her vision. But he put a finger on her lips, smiling. Then, suddenly, he was gone. Belle snuggled back into bed and slept soundly. Everything was all right. She would talk to Papa in the morning, after he had a night's rest.

The next morning, she dressed quickly and ran into the kitchen, where Mamma was putting wood on the fire. Her back was toward Belle, who asked, "When is Papa coming downstairs? I want to see him before I go to school."

Her mother turned around. "What are you talking about? You know your father is in Omaha."

"He came home last night. I saw him. He woke me up."

"Belle, what nonsense! You were dreaming."

"I wasn't, Mamma. I woke up and I saw him. He put his arms around me."

Mamma just shook her head. For a minute, Belle was angry. Everybody thought she was crazy, or making up things. Everybody but Papa. Then Jim and Hettie trooped into the kitchen and the baby started crying and Mamma sent her up to get little Gil. While she was upstairs, she opened the door of the room her parents slept in, quietly. More than anything, she hoped Papa would be there, still asleep. But the bed was empty.

She thought about Papa all day at school. Somehow, she felt sure that he would be home when she got there. So when school was out, she ran with Jim following her, Hettie and George, Jr., stumbling along more slowly. Jim wanted to stop to have a snowball fight, but Belle for once wasn't in the mood. She left him and ran into the kitchen.

Mamma was at the big round kitchen table, sitting with her head in her arms. She looked up at Belle, and Belle could see that Mamma had been crying.

Belle sat down at the table, dropping her books.

Mamma looked at her. "You saw your father last night. He came to tell you he was dying. You saw his ghost. He came to comfort you because he wanted you to be brave and help the rest of us. You should be very proud he chose you."

Belle said, "It wasn't his ghost. He was alive. I wasn't a bit frightened. If it had been a ghost, I would have been scared."

"He died last night around midnight. The man from the telegraph office at the railroad station rode out to tell me after you children had gone to school. Your father came in spirit to tell you not to grieve."

Belle started to cry. Her mother put a hand on her arm. "Not now, dearest. You must help me tell Jim and the others. They are bringing Papa home this afternoon. Some men will be bringing the body. We must have something for them to eat, and a hot drink."

Belle and Jim, as the two oldest, did their best to keep the younger children from being too miserable. And whenever Belle started to cry, Jim would put his arm around her and she would stop. When it came near time for the men to bring Papa, the two of them went to the front room to watch. They stood by the window holding hands, feeling miserable and yet grown-up. The cold wind came right through the heavy storm windows.

Finally they saw the horses and the sleigh on the road outside. They called Mamma. She came alone, leaving the other children in the kitchen. They watched the team turn into the driveway. There was no sound. The depth of the snow muffled all noise.

And Belle realized this was what she had seen back in July. She realized that spirits in the world beyond, where

Papa now lived, had opened the veil of mystery and allowed her a glimpse of the future. For everything was the same.

The man who ran the feed store was driving. Beside him on the box were the barber and the stationmaster of the railroad. Mr. Watts and his helper and the stranger were in the sleigh, balancing on its sides. And there was the coffin.

Then the men took it out of the sleigh and put it on their shoulders and brought it up the steps. Belle watched as much as she could. Finally she ran into her bedroom and threw herself down and cried. Yet, in a way, there was a comfort in knowing that a spirit world existed where she would be reunited with Papa.

Later that night, she learned who the stranger was. He was a salesman who had happened to come in to Le Mars on the same train that brought her father's body, and he had volunteered to help the local men carry the coffin.

Belle's own story was added to the family ghost stories. They all stayed on in Le Mars, and Mamma's brother and his wife came with their large family to help run the farm.

When Belle was seventeen, she became a milliner. In those days, ladies' hats were real creations, with lots of lace and feathers and ribbons. You couldn't find such hats in the usual small-town general stores. In fact, most of them were made by hand. Belle was clever with her needle and she studied magazines that came from New York with the latest fashions. So she went from town to town announcing her arrival in the local newspaper: "Madame Munro, with the latest fashions from New York and Paris in millinery."

She stayed at the local hotel, or in a genteel rooming house, and her hats were much in demand. So was Belle, for she was pretty, lively, and sure of herself. Going among strangers didn't bother her at all.

In Tecumseh, Nebraska, named after the chief of the Shawnee Indians who was defeated at the battle of Tippecanoe in 1811, she met a handsome veteran of the Civil War, Ernest Louis Roberts, who was a contractor with a brickyard. They fell in love and were married. He built most of the brick buildings that still stand on Main Street in that little town.

Belle had three daughters, one of whom was my mother. When the three girls married, they moved to Lincoln, about thirty miles away, the capital of Nebraska. When Ernest Roberts died, Grandma Belle also moved to Lincoln and built a small house near the three larger ones of her daughters. It was in that house where we children, her grandchildren, used to gather on cold nights to hear her tell ghost stories.

The tale of the coffin was the one we liked best. She told it so often that we could all repeat it by heart. I can to this day, as you have seen. But when it comes to the place where she recognizes the men on the sleigh, cold chills still go down my spine, because I know she was telling the truth.

There is just one more small footnote to her story. Through Grandma Belle, I had a small experience of my own with ghosts. Or at least I think I did. My mother always thought there was some logical explanation. She said, "Ghosts aren't *logical*."

When my father's business made it necessary for us to move to Chicago, Grandma Belle used to come and spend summers with us. I enjoyed having her. She was still as spunky and full of fun as ever, and she was a great tease. She thought most old people were bores. She confessed to me that even my own mother, her daughter, was a little square. She much preferred to spend her time with me and my school friends. She would tell them ghost stories and they loved them.

But as she grew older, and more and more crippled with arthritis, she decided maybe it wasn't right for her to repeat these tales. To this day, I don't know why. I can only guess that perhaps she felt the spirits in the world beyond didn't approve.

The summer after I graduated from high school, she came to visit us in Chicago for the last time. She was so lame she didn't even try to get in the car to go to church. The do-gooders at the Presbyterian church in our neighborhood who made a habit of visiting the sick tried to call on her. But she would peek out of her bedroom window and see them coming up the street and tell me not to answer the doorbell.

"Why should I bother with those old fogeys," she used to say to me. "I've little enough time left. I'm not going to be bored."

One afternoon, I was sitting in her bedroom with her. She couldn't leave it those days except to go to the dining room for meals, and that took a lot of pain and effort. The rest of the time, she lay in bed, her beautiful hair, white now, braided and pinned around her head. The heating lamp on her legs helped ease the pain. She almost never complained, but that day she said to me, "Drat, I'm sick of being old and crippled. One of these days, I'm going to give up and join Mamma and Papa and your Grandfather Ernest. To say nothing of little Jenny."

I asked, "Grandma Belle, when you are a ghost, will you pay me a visit?"

For a long while, she didn't answer. Then she said, "I'm not sure I would know how."

"But will you, if you can?"

"I wouldn't want to scare you."

I promised her I wouldn't be frightened, ever, of her.

She still shook her head and wouldn't let me bring up the subject again. And soon afterward she returned to Lincoln.

That fall, Grandma fell sick with pneumonia. My mother went to Lincoln to help her sisters take care of Grandma Belle, leaving my father and me alone in the apartment in Chicago.

One evening, Mother called to say Grandma Belle had died. I felt very sad. I sat by the telephone a long time after my father had gone into another room.

There was a pad of paper by the telephone, a pad where Mother used to write down messages and make grocery lists. I began absent-mindedly tearing off sheets, crumpling them and dropping them to the floor. By accident—or maybe it wasn't—I looked at one of them. It wasn't blank, like the others. It had a few words, in Grandma Belle's beautiful writing:

"My ghost had bright red hair and no limp."

My mother insisted that Grandma Belle had written the

message before she left, as a joke. But she had no explanation for what happened afterward.

I felt a hand on my shoulder. It gave me a push and I tumbled off the telephone chair and landed smack on the floor. And I could hear Grandma Belle laughing.

My mother said that was just my imagination. But she was wrong. Grandma Belle had paid me a visit. But she has never come back. Even though I wasn't a bit afraid at the time and wouldn't be again.

Chapter 2
GHOSTLY- AND GHASTLY- DOGS

Grandma Belle had a story about a ghost dog. A major, a strange old man, told his wife that when he died he was going to come back and haunt her in the shape of his dog, a black water spaniel. It was going to be his revenge. For his wife hated dogs and never allowed the spaniel in the house.

After he died, she had the spaniel destroyed. That was the end of that, she told the local people.

Shortly afterward, she noticed the smell of dog in the house. She sprayed and sprayed, but it grew stronger. Next, dirty paw marks appeared in the kitchen, on her rugs. One night, as she was going to bed, she saw a pair of furry legs climbing in beside her.

Next morning she was found dead in bed, with two black paw marks on her throat. The doctor said she must have died of fright.

Dogs may seem almost human to us when they are loved family pets. But they are, after all, animals. When dogs are deserted by their owners, left to roam the streets or countryside, they can become vicious. Some of them have joined packs that attack other animals and have killed people.

So it isn't surprising to find ghost dogs, under certain circumstances, being dangerous.

A writer named Peter rented a house in a French village. He wanted peace and quiet to finish a book. He also found a competent older woman to live in and cook and clean for him.

One day, going down the stairs from his bedroom, he saw a big black dog at the foot of the stairs. He spoke to it, thinking it had wandered in by mistake. The dog growled at him menacingly. Then he noticed something peculiar. The dog had only three legs. One of its hind legs was missing. He called for the maid to come and bring a broom, to scare the animal away. Before his eyes, the dog vanished.

After that he heard the dog limping up the stairs. Sometimes he felt a furry form brush past him. The people next door told him that the tenants before him had left their dog to roam the countryside for food. He caught his leg in a trap. When he was found, he had died of starvation, but before that he had almost chewed his leg off, trying to get free.

Peter was just as glad the dog stayed invisible. But one morning the maid told him she wouldn't sleep in the house any longer. The night before, the black dog had limped into her room and put his head on her bed. His muzzle was covered with blood, and blood oozed out of his mouth.

Peter wasn't too happy about being alone in the house. So he borrowed two German shepherd dogs from the local priest. They were big, powerful dogs. He took them up to his bedroom with him.

In the middle of the night, he woke up. The shepherds were growling. He put on the light. The door opened slowly. Suddenly, the two shepherds were lunging and howling at something he could not see. One leaped in the air and fell to the floor, bleeding terribly from a gash in its throat. The other ran under the bed, howling.

It was daylight before Peter dared to get out of bed. One of the shepherd dogs was dead, and the other was in a state of shock, cowering and trembling.

Peter didn't wait to see what happened next. He packed his things and was gone before nightfall.

But what would you do if the ghost of a dog you had loved came back and attacked you? That is just what happened to a girl named Jenny.

Jenny lived with her parents and sister, Carol, in Vermont, on a farm that bordered a big pond. One winter day the pond was frozen over and Jenny was ice-skating on it. Near the edge, she spotted what seemed to be a little ball of fur. It was a tiny puppy, lying half-frozen in the snow.

Although Jenny was not yet fourteen, she had already

decided she was going to be a nurse. She brought the puppy home, wrapped it in blankets, and fed it warm milk from an eye dropper. Soon the puppy was alert, begging for food. It ate until its little belly popped out. So she named it Henry, after the fat English king Henry the Eighth.

Henry grew up to be a big, gaunt yellow dog, a fierce fighter. He had a ferocious bark and he bit more than one tramp before Jenny's father fenced in the yard and put up a sign, "Beware the Dog." He had whipped all the other farm dogs for miles around, and somewhere along the line most of one ear had been chewed off. This, and his battle-scarred muzzle, didn't improve his appearance.

But he adored Jenny. She could do anything with him, even make him stop fighting and come home. One word from her and he turned into a lap dog.

Jenny's mother wanted to get rid of him. No matter how many times she shut him in the kitchen at night, when morning came she would find him in Jenny's bedroom, on the foot of her bed. Jenny's older sister, Carol, hated the beast. He used to snarl at her beau. One night, when they were dancing to the radio, Henry came in and jumped on the beau and tore one pant leg almost off him.

But Henry had a friend in Jenny's father. Jenny's father admired Henry's free spirit. When spring was in the air, Henry managed to dig his way out of the fenced-in yard and go courting. Every summer, there were lots of puppies around that looked like Henry. Besides, Henry was the best watchdog imaginable. With him around, nobody would dare touch Jenny. And since Carol was going to be married soon, and Jenny would often be alone when her parents were away, it was good to have him protecting her.

Henry was four years old when Jenny left home to go to nursing school in Boston. She hated to leave him, but her father told her not to worry, he'd take good care of the dog.

"We understand each other because we both love you," he said.

Everything went well until Jenny was in her junior year at the nursing school. Then Carol's husband was killed in an accident, leaving Carol with a tiny baby who had been born prematurely. Carol came home to the farm, bringing little Nicole with her.

"You have to get rid of that terrible dog," she told Jenny. "He might hurt Nicole."

Jenny took Henry aside and talked to him for a long time. She told him his fate hung in the balance. Whether he understood the words she said or not, he got the message.

He adopted the baby. He slept under her carriage when her mother put her out in the yard. In the house, he padded around after the baby, watching her being bathed and put to bed. At night, when the baby was put into her crib, he insisted on staying in the room with her until it was time for Carol to go to bed. It was funny, a family joke—until one night.

Carol had just tucked the baby in and joined her parents in the living room when Henry appeared, barking. Carol told him to keep still, he would wake Nicole.

But Henry's barking became more urgent.

Jenny's father said, "Carol, he's trying to tell us something. Go and look at the baby."

Carol went in and found little Nicole had almost smothered in her blankets. Her face had already turned blue. A few minutes more and she would have been dead.

After that, Henry could do no wrong. "He saved my baby's life," Carol would say. "Nicole wouldn't be here if it weren't for Henry."

Nicole learned to walk holding on to Henry's stubby tail. No matter how hard she hit him, he always turned the other cheek.

"He's an angel," she told Jenny.

But Henry wasn't an angel. One spring day, the old urge to get out and sow a few wild oats came to him. He dug his way out under the fence. He was chasing chickens and ducks when the farmer next door shot him.

The farmer told Jenny's father, "The damned dog was a killer. Everybody knows that."

The whole family mourned Henry, even Jenny's mother. "I miss him," she admitted. "He wasn't such a bad old dog, after all."

Jenny was graduating in June. Her parents had given her money for a trip to San Francisco as a present. One day she passed a pet shop in Boston and stopped, as usual, to watch the puppies in the window. One looked exactly like a little teddy bear. He had bright brown shoe-button eyes, and one ear flopped over.

She couldn't resist going in the shop. The owner told her the puppy was a Norwegian elkhound, one of the oldest breeds in Scandinavia, dating back to the days of the Vikings. The breed was not much known in America, but the dogs were famous in Europe for their loyalty and courage.

She played with the puppy, then put him back in the window. She didn't want another dog. Her heart still belonged to old Henry.

Just before graduation, she went by the shop again.

The little elkhound was still there. She went in again. The dog looked at her wistfully. The pet-shop owner explained that the puppy was hard to sell because he had a long pedigree, was of a rare breed, and was expensive.

"How much?" Jenny asked.

"I'll let you have him for two hundred dollars," he said.

Two hundred dollars! It was a large part of the money Jenny had been given for her trip. But the puppy cuddled down in her arms and looked at her as though it was all settled. She went back to the dormitory and got the money. She named the puppy Cisco, for he represented her trip to San Francisco.

When fall came, she had to leave Cisco at the farm. She had a job in a New York hospital and was going to live in the nurse's residence. But she promised Cisco she would soon find an apartment where she could keep him. Cisco was very different from Henry. He was cute and lovable and friendly. In fact, he was so friendly he was a terrible watchdog. Jenny's father said if a burglar wanted to come in, Cisco would wag his tail and show him around the house.

Finally Jenny found an apartment in an old house on Twenty-eighth Street, right across from the hospital. It was one room on the first floor, over a laundry in the basement. But it was perfect because it was a big room with french doors that opened into a little backyard. When she was at work, she could leave the doors open and Cisco could go down and play in the yard. There was such a tall fence around it that it was perfectly safe.

She went home at Christmas and brought Cisco back with her on the plane. He loved New York and people loved him, he was so cute. Jenny made a lot of friends through the puppy. One was a Dr. Finch, who had his veterinary practice on nearby Second Avenue and lived above his office. He knew the breed and assured Jenny that Cisco was a particularly fine elkhound. She was very proud of him.

But in late March and early April, something happened to Cisco. From a happy, bounding puppy, he changed into a frightened, cowering creature. He was afraid to go down two steps to the yard. When she picked him up and put him in the yard, he stood there trembling, begging her to take him back in the house. And when she was gone, he tore up her shoes, ate the lining of the carpet, even opened the refrigerator and pulled food out on the floor.

She took him to Dr. Finch. He examined him carefully. Finally he said, "Jenny, there is nothing wrong with him physically. But something has killed his spirit. He's nervous and scared. Why don't you let me take him upstairs for a couple of days, and my wife and I will watch him and see if we can spot the trouble?"

Jenny agreed. The first night she was alone without Cisco, she had a funny dream. Henry was standing by her bed, watching her. For some reason, she was afraid. Then she woke up and, of course, nobody was there. But it stayed with her all day.

So that evening, when she went off duty at the hospital, she went to Dr. Finch's. She said she'd decided she wanted Cisco home.

"He's been fine," Dr. Finch told her. "At first he was a little timid but he got over that. Jenny, there may be something around your apartment that has scared him. Let me come over after office hours, about ten o'clock."

Cisco seemed delighted to see Jenny. But as soon as

they got back to her apartment, he became nervous. She changed her uniform for blue jeans and a sweater and fixed dinner for them both. Then she settled down on the daybed to read. Cisco was restless, moving around the apartment, sniffing at the doors, once in a while giving a miserable little whine. She picked him up and settled him on the daybed beside her. Usually, because he was such a furry little animal, he liked to sleep on the floor where it was cool, or in the bathroom. But tonight he couldn't get close enough to her.

Outside, a dog howled. Cisco shuddered. And Jenny shuddered, too. Because it was old Henry. Jenny would have recognized his howl anywhere. It was the way he had always sounded when he came home after one of his sprees and wanted to be let in—mournful yet demanding. "Hurry up," the howl said, "don't keep me waiting."

She picked up Cisco. He let out a yelp and ran to the bathroom. Jenny felt cold. But she said to herself, aloud, "There is nothing to be frightened about. If it's Henry's ghost, I'm going to be glad to see him. He may be jealous of Cisco. But I'll explain I missed him so much I had to have another puppy."

She opened the french doors. Although the night was warm, she shivered.

Henry was standing in the backyard. The same old Henry, with his scarred muzzle and battered ear. She spoke to him quietly, calling his name. He wagged the yellow stub of a tail.

Quietly again, she lowered herself on the first step that went down to the yard. Henry growled, low, menacing.

She said, "Henry, it's Jenny. You've come to see me, I know. Well, here I am. I'm not afraid."

He lunged at her.

It was the most terrible moment of her life. She flung out one arm and his teeth sank into it. Then she kicked out and caught him, hurling him back down into the yard. Before he could attack again, she ran inside and shut the doors, trembling all over.

While she was catching her breath, something brushed against her legs. She screamed. But it was only Cisco, looking to her for comfort. She leaned down and picked him up. He was trembling harder than she was.

"I'll get you out," she told him. "Forgive me. He's been around, scaring the life out of you while I was gone. I didn't understand."

She started toward the front door. It was no use.

Henry appeared between it and them. His jaws were open, his lips drawn back, and his long canine teeth gleamed like fangs. She thought of the farmer who had shot Henry. He'd said, "That dog's a killer." And she wondered, dully, if Henry was going to kill her and Cisco, too.

At that moment, when she couldn't seem to move, Cisco came to life. He growled courageously. Henry made a leap for him and Cisco jumped out of Jenny's arms and ran underneath the daybed. Henry was after him in a moment. The most unearthly noises came from underneath the couch, high-pitched howls that sounded like human screaming. Jenny was sure Cisco was being killed.

She picked up the first thing her hand touched, a floor lamp, and hurled it at the yellow legs that were protruding beyond the couch. A yelp—that was Henry. Ghost or not, he could still feel pain.

Anger took hold of her. She was beyond being afraid

now. She only wanted to save Cisco. She picked up a metal ashtray and ran over to the couch, beating hard on Henry's legs, blind with fury. She didn't realize it, but she must have been screaming. For a voice beyond the door finally cut through to her consciousness.

"Jenny, is that you? Answer me, or I'll knock down the door."

She recognized Dr. Finch's voice. Sanity returned. She answered him and stumbled to the door.

"Save Cisco. Henry's going to kill him. Do something. Please—"

Dr. Finch came back into the room with her. They looked down where Henry had been. There was blood on the rug. There was the broken lamp and the ashtray. But Henry had gone. There were no yellow legs. From underneath the couch, Cisco was whining.

He was still alive. But his throat had been torn open and one paw was badly chewed. Dr. Finch was fearful that there might be internal injuries, so they made a stretcher out of a blanket and carried Cisco through the street to his office. Then Dr. Finch called his wife and asked her to take care of Jenny while he got Cisco ready for surgery.

Jenny sat in his waiting room, head in hands, until Mrs. Finch arrived. She swept into the room, and took charge. Her first words were, "Child, you're bleeding. Do you know you're hurt? I'm going to take you over to the emergency room at the hospital."

As it turned out, Jenny had been bitten both on the arm and on the leg. Her sweater was torn, but Henry's teeth had gone through her blue jeans without breaking the material. The young resident in charge knew Jenny.

He said, "Those are pretty bad bites. Who did it? Your own dog?"

Jenny nodded. He had to cauterize the wounds and that stung.

"Did your dog have all its shots? I'll have to report this to the police. You might have to have rabies treatments if he didn't."

Jenny nodded again. What did it matter if a ghost dog had his shots or not? And could you catch rabies from a ghost?

"Well, let me tell you this, young lady. You'll be okay, but I think you should stay off that leg for a few days. As for that dog of yours, he's vicious. You should get rid of him. Why don't you have something nice and gentle like a tiger for a pet next time?"

Mrs. Finch went home with her and cleaned up the apartment. Jenny watched her, drinking hot tea, telling the whole story.

Finally Mrs. Finch said, "I don't believe in ghosts. Just the same, some mean dog got in here and I don't want you to be alone. Can you get somebody to stay with you?"

Jenny's sister, Carol, had been wanting to come to New York. So Jenny called her, explaining that she was taking a few days off—she didn't say why—and would like company. Carol agreed to catch a plane and be there that evening.

Mrs. Finch went back home after fixing Jenny's breakfast. Soon Dr. Finch was at the door, with the good news that Cisco would be all right.

"It will take a week or two before he can come home. Being under the couch saved him from being killed, or having his back broken. But how can we fix it so this won't happen again?"

"You know it was a ghost dog?"

"My wife told me." Dr. Finch was silent. "I think you should get out of here."

"He came through the door when it was closed. He left the same way. If he wants to, he can follow us anyplace."

"Then maybe you should get rid of Cisco. If that is why your old dog is bothering you. You do believe it was your old dog?"

"I recognized him."

Dr. Finch shook his head. "I don't have any answers. But I'm glad you won't be alone. That sister of yours is a pretty sensible girl, I hope."

Jenny nodded. He still didn't believe her. Well, it was a pretty farfetched tale.

When Carol arrived, she had little Nicole with her. Little Nicole, now two and a half, was a darling brown-eyed girl. But for once, Jenny wasn't glad to see her.

"What if Henry should hurt her? Oh, Carol, I wouldn't want anything to happen that would even scare her."

Carol said briskly, "Don't talk nonsense. I know Henry would never hurt her. Remember how he saved her life? Besides, I think you are imagining ghosts. Some horrible tramp dog got in."

"But how?"

"Through the fence. Or something. Stop being so jumpy. Before I leave, I'll have the yard examined and the hole plugged up. Now let's have some fun while I'm here."

And they did. Jenny couldn't walk far with her leg, but

she stayed home with Nicole while Carol shopped and went to museums. Nicole was a darling, into everything, and it was a good tonic for Jenny to have her mind and hands occupied. But after two days of baby-sitting, Jenny had exhausted the games and stories she knew. Besides, she'd had one or two odd experiences.

Once she looked out and saw Cisco's jingle ball in the middle of the backyard. He had been playing with it in the kitchen the night he was attacked. How could it have got out into the yard?

Then she began to notice an indentation on the foot of her bed, as though a dog had been lying there. She would straighten out the cover, and the indentation would be there again.

Most important, the apartment seemed chilly all the time. When Nicole was asleep, Jenny said to her sister, "I have the feeling Henry is hanging around, watching us. I wish you hadn't brought Nicole. What if he should attack her?"

"Jenny," Carol said, "you're getting the whim-whams, being shut in like this. Take Nicole out tomorrow. There's a park two blocks up. Go and sit in the sunshine and let her play with other kids."

So the next morning, Jenny and Nicole started out. It was a warm, sunny day. Outside, they happened to meet Mrs. Finch, who was on her way to her volunteer job at the hospital. She stopped to admire Nicole and then reported that Cisco was on the mend. At the moment, he was sleeping in the sun in her kitchen, on a bed she'd made for him of old sheets. She thought that by tomorrow he might be glad to see Jenny and Nicole.

Jenny was so pleased with the good news about her dog that she didn't realize Nicole had let go of her hand. Her first sign that Nicole had slipped away was a scream of brakes in the street and a car stopping shudderingly. Mrs. Finch screamed.

Then a man leaped out of the car and picked little Nicole up from the curb. She was all right, except that her dress was dirty and her face was scratched.

He said, "I couldn't help it, lady. The little girl stepped right out in the street in front of the car. Thank God for the dog. He came out of nowhere and picked her up by her skirt and threw her into the curb. Otherwise I might have killed her."

Nicole said indignantly, "The doggie hurt me. Naughty doggie."

The driver of the car said, "I'm afraid I killed your dog. He saved the little girl, but I hit him full on. I could feel the wheels passing over him. But he died a hero. I'll get a policeman and see that they take care of the body. You shouldn't look at it."

Nicole was crying now, beginning to be scared. Jenny took her in her arms, although she was shaking herself. She started back into the apartment. Then she turned around and handed Nicole to Mrs. Finch.

"I have to look at him," she said. "I have to say good-bye."

She went over to the curb. But there was no dog, no body, not even a drop of blood on the street.

The driver said, "I saw him. As plain as day. A great big yellow dog. It was almost human, the way he picked up the little girl and threw her out of my way. I didn't dream it."

"No," Jenny said. "You didn't dream it. That was our dog. He saved the baby's life once before. This time—well, he'd done something bad. I think he was trying to make up for it."

"He must have run away. I hope he comes back."

"I don't think he will." Jenny looked at the stranger's white face. "Don't worry. He's better off where he is."

"Can't I put an ad in the paper for him?"

Jenny shook her head. "No. I'm sure he doesn't want to come back. Not now. You see, he was a ghost. He was hanging around because he was unhappy. But I think he's learned his lesson."

"Lady, are you all right?"

Jenny started to say of course. Then she saw Henry. He had crawled out from underneath the car. He was standing there, wagging his tail at her as fast as the yellow stub could move.

She said, "Don't you see him? There, in front of your car?"

The man turned around. Henry's big mouth was open but his lips weren't drawn back. He seemed to be laughing at them. And then he vanished, melted into the sunlight.

"I must be going crazy," the driver said. "Or else I've seen a ghost."

"He came to say good-bye," Jenny told him, and went back into her apartment to have a good cry.

Chapter 3
SATAN'S KINGDOM

Certain Irish families, like the O'Rourkes and the O'Donnells and the O'Neills, are supposed to have ghosts that follow them wherever they go. I never knew that, until Auntie Boo came to live next door to us in Chicago. She wasn't my real aunt. She was the maiden aunt of Dr. O'Rourke, our family doctor, whom everybody loved because he was so kind and jolly. He was a big man with prematurely white hair who looked like Santa Claus. His wife had died when she was having a baby and Auntie Boo had come to help him take care of Carl, the baby, and Kathleen, who was five at the time, a year older than I.

Just as Grandma Belle told me and my cousins Scottish ghost stories, Auntie Boo stuffed us kids with tales of

Irish ghosts. Banshees were always in the form of women. They could be young and beautiful or old and ugly, gleeful or hellish. But a visit from a banshee always meant somebody in the household was going to die. They howled and screamed, clapped their hands or laughed diabolically. They were cause enough for fright. But even worse were the elementals, because they were neither human being nor animal, a strange mixture of both and something else horrible. Once you ever looked one in the face, you were aware that it came from the worst and most wholly evil side of the unknown.

"Have you ever seen an elemental?" Carl once asked Auntie Boo.

She crossed herself. "The good Lord forbid. When my time comes, the O'Rourke banshee will appear. But I never in my life want to meet an elemental. I would die of fright on the spot."

Dr. O'Rourke used to tease Auntie Boo about the banshee coming for her. But even he didn't make jokes about elementals. Once I heard him talking to my father about them. "Being a medical man," he said, "I must say we have no proof that they exist. I just hope they don't. For, from the old stories I've had repeated to me, they are so utterly evil they can charm the senses out of any human being or animal, make them do dreadful things. Only cats are immune."

We used to have Dr. O'Rourke over at the house a lot for parties, because my mother was trying to find a wife for him.

"Those children need a real mother," she used to tell him. "You and Auntie Boo spoil them."

And he'd answer, "Why not? They're all we have."

But my mother insisted that the children needed discipline. Carl was a handsome little boy, but he was always playing practical jokes, and sometimes the jokes were mean, like the time he cut off one of my pigtails and my mother had to cut off the other, leaving me looking like a skinned duck. Kathleen, on the other hand, could be sweet as pie—so long as she had her own way. She'd get mad if you crossed her, and impose a "rule of silence," which meant that none of the other kids were supposed to speak to you.

Mother kept producing possible wives for the doctor. Some were widows with children of their own, and others were just single women. He kept insisting he had to devote his life to Carl and Kathleen until Mother had an inspiration and produced my old kindergarten teacher, Miss Ames, Miss Hannah Ames. Hannah, as we all called her behind her back, had a way with kids. We were crazy about her. She was a big woman who had been raised on a farm with dozens of brothers and sisters, and she could do almost anything. But she never stood for any nonsense. If you got out of line, you got told off.

Hannah had never had much time for men. She'd made up her mind not to marry, but when the doctor proposed, she had a change of heart. She cried when she told my mother she was going to get married. And the doctor was equally happy. "How could I resist anyone so good and kind?" he said.

Carl and Kathleen weren't quite so happy. Nor was Auntie Boo. But the three of them hid their displeasure because, as Kathleen told me, their father might have picked someone a lot worse. "We can push Hannah around." (Not having had Hannah as a teacher, Carl and Kathleen didn't know, as I did, that Hannah had a mind of her own.) Then Kathleen added, "But how would you feel if your mother died and your father brought a strange woman home to take her place?" I tried to say how much I liked Hannah, but I realized how hard it was, especially for Kathleen. Carl hadn't really ever known his own mother.

Soon after Hannah and the doctor were married, he took a job with an insurance company in Hartford, Connecticut. "I think a change will do us all good," he told my mother. "We'll start fresh. And Hannah won't be moving into another woman's house. I've bought a place in the country, and she can fix it up just the way she wants. She's never had a place of her own."

The area where he had bought the house was called Satan's Kingdom. When I asked why, Kathleen told me with a superior air, "It's just one of those quaint old New England names."

They moved into the new place in the summer. Almost right away, things began to go wrong. The three-story house was built into a big boulder of black rock, which formed one wall. A Boston architect had built it for his wife, but she had died shortly after they moved in and he wanted no part of the place.

Hannah furnished the living room and dining room with her old family pieces, marble-top tables and Victorian chairs and sofas. In the dining room was an old mission set that her grandparents had used. And the bedroom she and the doctor shared had a rosewood carved bed with matching dresser and dressing table. Hannah loved to sew, so she made all the draperies and curtains and the bedspread herself. She also had some beautiful old porcelain vases that her grandfather had brought from China, where he had been a missionary. She made these into lamps.

But she left the kitchen to Auntie Boo. In it were her favorite pots and pans, arranged the way Auntie Boo liked them, and Auntie Boo's old rocker was placed near the window, where she could look out over the fields. They really had no one living near them, except a man who raised vicious dogs for guard duty, mastiffs. The house and kennel had signs warning people to stay away.

Hannah also put the furniture the doctor and his dead wife had used in Auntie Boo's bedroom, which was on the second floor, as was the one she shared with the doctor. And on the third floor, where the children's bedrooms were, she let them have exactly the furniture they wanted, from the old apartment. She had done her best not to make Auntie Boo or the children feel she was trying to make over their lives.

But neither Carl nor Kathleen nor Auntie Boo was really happy. It was all so different.

The children liked the local school all right. Carl was good at sports and was soon on the various teams. And Kathleen got into dramatics and joined the drama club. With her mother's red hair and dark eyes, Kathleen was a real Irish beauty, and the drama teacher cast her in a starring role in the next play. But they missed their old friends. And Carl began walking in his sleep, something he hadn't done since he was a small boy.

One morning, Auntie Boo went down to fix breakfast and she saw Carl outside, asleep under a tree. It was October and already there had been a frost. He caught a bad cold. She said to Hannah, "You must keep your bedroom door

open and watch for the child. It won't be my fault if he gets pneumonia."

Then the furnace didn't work right. Hannah thought maybe that was because the house had been built into a rock. She would be upstairs sewing and it would be so hot she had to open the windows. Then when she went downstairs to the kitchen Auntie Boo would be bundled up in sweaters, wearing gloves, trying to peel potatoes. And there were cold spots in the house, in the most unlikely places. The coldest was in the kitchen, where Auntie Boo's rocker stood. When she wanted to sit down and have a nice cup of tea, she used to have to wrap up in a blanket.

"I hate this house," she said to Hannah. "We never should have left Chicago."

Hannah also began to get her back up. So far, she had been careful to keep away from the kitchen, to let Auntie Boo plan the menus. Hannah did the marketing but Auntie Boo told her what to buy. Hannah cleaned and swept and washed up, but Auntie Boo cooked the way she always had, and the food was too starchy for Hannah. She felt she and the doctor should have more vegetables and salads. But she said nothing—yet.

Then she began to feel Auntie Boo was spying on her. It was an ugly feeling. She would be making beds. The doctor was at his office; the children were in school. She would hear footsteps on the stairs, pausing outside the door of the room where she was working. Then nothing. She would call out, "Auntie Boo, don't just stand there. Come in, if you want something." But nothing. And if she hurried outside, nobody was ever there.

"I'm doing my best," she told the doctor. "But I'm afraid the poor soul can't accept me."

Hannah didn't know—and the doctor didn't know how to tell her—that Auntie Boo was complaining to him about Hannah. "I think she is trying to drive me crazy. When everybody is asleep, she comes down to the kitchen and mixes up my supplies. She put salt in my sugar container. If I hadn't tasted the lemon pie I made for dinner last night before I served it, you would have all thought I was ready for the nut house. I'd made it with salt instead of sugar."

One night when Hannah went down to set the table for breakfast, she found Auntie Boo collapsed in the kitchen. A bottle of cooking sherry was on the sink, almost empty.

"For all our sakes," she told the doctor, "you have to speak to her."

The next morning the doctor went in to see Auntie Boo. She was still in bed, saying she had caught cold. She looked white and very old.

"The banshee came for me when I was fixing dinner last night. I'm scared."

"What happened?" The doctor sat down by her bed and took her hand.

"It—she was a young woman, with beautiful red hair, hair like Kathleen's. She wept something awful. My time has come."

"Now, Auntie Boo, there's nothing wrong with you except maybe you're working too hard. Why don't you let Hannah help you in the kitchen? She says I'm getting too fat on your good cooking, anyway."

Auntie Boo started to cry. "She's trying to drive me crazy. You don't understand. I guess that's what the banshee meant. If I don't get out of here, I'm going to die."

The doctor gave Auntie Boo an injection to help her sleep. But when he got home from work that night, Auntie Boo was dressed in her hat and coat, sitting in the living room with bags and bundles around her. She insisted that the doctor drive her to the bus. "I'm going to go live with the nuns. If I spend another night in this house I'll die."

When the doctor came back from the depot, Hannah put his dinner on the table. The children had already eaten. He pushed the plate aside and went and poured himself a glass of whiskey.

"Hannah," he said, "have either you or the children been trying to scare Auntie Boo? She's an old woman and set in her ways. But she came and helped me out at a time when I needed her very much. I wouldn't like to feel we're turning her out of the only home she's ever known."

Hannah had been patient. She had been careful not to complain to the doctor about the way the children ignored her and did only what Auntie Boo told them. She had even tried to accept Auntie Boo's starchy cooking. But enough was enough.

"Maybe it was a mistake to have married me," she said and stood up, her cheeks red. The doctor took her in his arms. "Don't be angry, Hannah. It's just—well, I was upset, watching that poor old woman get on the bus alone. Maybe she will be better off with the nuns."

That night, all was quiet. But in a few days, everything got worse.

Carl's sleepwalking was no longer just a nuisance. He began doing naughty things. They were all directed against his stepmother. He smashed one of her favorite lamps. He'd leave the freezer open. Meats would be defrosting in the middle of the white damask sofa that had belonged to Hannah's mother. A plate that Hannah's kindergarten class had given her as a wedding present was found smashed in the fireplace. One morning she came downstairs and found he had pulled everything off the kitchen shelves. Flour and catsup and syrup and all sorts of other things were lying in a sticky mess in the middle of the kitchen floor. She thought he should be punished.

The doctor said, "Hannah, the boy doesn't know what he is doing. He is walking in his sleep."

"I can't believe it. I think he wants to show he hates me. He pretends he is alseep, for he is doing what he wouldn't dare to do if he were awake."

The doctor hadn't been sleeping well. He felt guilty about Auntie Boo, and about Hannah, too. But it was hard to scold his son for actions done while sleepwalking.

He said, "Please try to be patient. If there is too much work for you, we can hire a maid."

Hannah had reached the end of her patience. "I don't need a maid," she shouted. "I need some consideration from you and your children."

He left the house without saying good-bye. But by the end of the day he was sorry. He brought home a big box of roses for Hannah. She wasn't in the kitchen. Carl and Kathleen were alone there, eating cookies. They told him Hannah was upstairs in the bedroom.

He tried to open the door. It was locked. She called out she didn't want to see him, she wanted to think things out. He threw the roses in the garbage can.

The doctor spent a miserable night in Auntie Boo's bed. He tossed and turned. Once he thought he saw somebody standing by the door. Thinking it was Hannah, he sat up and turned on the light.

A slender figure, dressed all in black, her face covered with a black veil, was watching him. Although he couldn't see her face, he was sure she was smiling at him. His heart turned over. Her hair was red and curly, like Kathleen's. Like Kathleen's mother's. He said, "Come closer."

When she obeyed, he smelled the most enchanting perfume of a delicate, unearthly sweetness. It made him dizzy. She held out two soft white hands, far softer and more delicious than any hands he had ever seen. He tried to take them in his, and she vanished.

He jumped out of bed. He flung open the closed door. She was floating down the steps to the front door. As he looked, she turned and held out her arms.

All reason left him. He dressed quickly in the clothes he had tossed off the night before. She was waiting for him by the front door. But when he appeared, she vanished again. He felt a blast of the coldest air imaginable. It was winter, and snowing outside. But this was a chill from a tomb.

He grabbed his storm coat. He didn't wait to put on his galoshes. He ran outside. It was snowing hard. But he could see her in the distance.

Like a man in a spell, he followed. He fell in drifts. But he got up and stumbled on. His bare hands were freez-

ing. Snow beat on his head. His glasses got fogged. His feet were soaked. His toes were numb.

At the foot of the hill, just as he was ready to catch up with her, she vanished again. He felt hopeless; he felt that if he didn't find her he didn't want to live. There were lights in the tavern that catered to truck drivers. He went up on the porch and peered in. He thought he saw her sitting in a back booth. But when he got inside, he saw it was only a coat belonging to a trucker who was sitting on a stool, drinking coffee.

He stared at the doctor. "Man, you're in awful shape. You look as though you'd seen a ghost. You need something stronger than coffee. Have a drink."

The doctor knew he needed coffee. But when the waitress came over, he ordered whiskey.

Toward morning, he stumbled into the house. Hannah turned away from the window, where she'd been watching him come up the hill. "I guess what you did last night is my answer. I'm leaving. I'll take a small bag. When I know where I'll be living, I'll send for the rest of my things."

He offered to drive her, but she said he was in no shape. She called a taxi. When it came, he carried her bag out and fell in a drift. This time it was Hannah who left without saying good-bye. Her wedding ring was on the dresser in their bedroom.

But he felt a strange sensation of relief. Now he and the children were alone.

Alone with the ghost. For he knew that was what she was.

Up until then, Kathleen had enjoyed the excitement of the commotion in the house. She had loved Auntie Boo, but it was easier without her telling Kathleen what to do. As for Hannah, she didn't really belong in the family. She wasn't their mother.

But she soon found out that she had more on her hands than she really wanted. She not only had Carl. She had a strange man who didn't act at all like her father.

The morning after Hannah left, he called his office to say he had the flu and wouldn't be in for a few days. Then he went to the kitchen, had a big drink of whiskey, and went upstairs to bed.

Carl said, "Now we can do anything we want. First of all, I'm not going to school."

Kathleen started to protest. She decided it would do no good. Her father wouldn't care. And without him, she had no authority over her brother. She stayed home, too.

The first day was horrible. But it was better than the nightmare that followed. Her father was like a zombie. For a few minutes a day, he seemed normal. He got up, shaved and dressed, and drank black coffee. He talked to his office, saying he still was sick. Afterward he drove to the village to shop. He brought home canned food and hot dogs for Carl and Kathleen, and whiskey for himself.

Then he would shut himself in the bedroom.

Carl was completely out of hand. He ran around in his dirty night clothes. He wouldn't bathe. He left dirty dishes around. Right after Kathleen washed the dishes, he would come out and make a fresh mess, spilling food all over the kitchen.

They got mice. Kathleen hated mice. She opened the door and coaxed an old tomcat in to chase them away. Carl got a pail of water and started to drown the cat.

Kathleen hid the poor old tom in her room. Then she marched downstairs, fire in her eyes.

"Carl, you've got to shape up. Daddy's gone off his rocker. We have to keep our heads."

Carl laughed. "Says who? You can't make me do anything. Just try."

She gave up. Everything went to pieces. Dirty glasses and dishes were all over the house, even on the stairs. Nobody picked them up. Her father ignored them. Carl kicked them when he was walking in his sleep. She no longer listened for her brother or tried to get him back to bed without waking him. She just didn't care what happened to any of them.

She took to staying in her room, reading or listening to the radio. The cat seemed altogether terrified. He wouldn't go out of her room, even when the door was open. Once when Kathleen came back with food, he even hissed at her.

One morning she woke up in cold panic. She looked at her messy room and realized she was getting as bad as Carl and her father. If this went on, they would all destroy themselves.

But she did not know what to do. She dreaded going into the tavern, for it was always filled with strangers. The only person living nearby was the man who raised guard dogs, which made terrible noises when she and Carl walked near his place. For the first time in her life, she wished she had been nicer to Hannah. Hannah might help her even now. But where was she? And she couldn't call the insurance company and get her father into trouble.

She decided to make one last effort to get through to the doctor. She waited for the time in the day when he dressed and had his coffee before calling the office. She went downstairs. Although her father's hand shook and he'd cut himself while shaving, he was sober.

"Daddy, I'm worried about Carl. He won't go to school and I have to stay home to watch him. He's being mean and nasty."

Her father put down his cup. He would not look at her. "I'm sorry, daughter. In a few days, I'll feel better. Then I'll talk to Carl."

"Daddy, you must talk to him now."

"Why?"

"He's getting horrid. I think there is something evil in this house. That's why Auntie Boo and Hannah left."

He stood up. For the first time, her father looked old to her. "Dear heart, don't push me. I have things on my mind."

She waited until he had taken the car out of the garage and started toward the village. Then she went up and found Hannah's address book. She began calling people who might know where Hannah was. She was so intent on what she was doing that she didn't hear the car return or the front door open. Until her father shouted, "I told you not to push me!"

He grabbed the telephone out of her hands and ripped the cord from the wall.

She fled up to her bedroom. She flung herself against the stone wall screaming, beating on it until her hands were bloody. After a long time, she sank exhausted to the floor. The old cat came over, sniffed at her, and crawled into her lap.

She decided she must find a way of making her brother realize how bad the situation was. She went downstairs.

Carl, still in his dirty night clothes, was cooking up one of his messes. The smell was horrible.

She said, "Carl, we've got to escape. Something horrible has happened to Daddy. If we don't get help, he'll die."

He kept his back to her. "Don't be such a jerk. You and I could have fun if you didn't shut yourself in your room with that old cat."

"I'm not going to any longer. I'm going to the police."

Carl tasted what he'd put in the pot. "Stop being such a square."

"Is it square to mind that Daddy is drunk all the time? And won't eat? If we don't do something, he'll die."

That got his attention. He turned around. "Then it will be you and me. We'll manage."

"Manage? Don't be silly. They'll put us in an orphanage. We'll have to scrub floors. And eat bread and water. And they'll beat us. Every day. Especially on Christmas."

Carl looked doubtful. "You're kidding."

"Or maybe they'll put Daddy in an asylum. Would you like that?"

"What can we do?"

She didn't answer right away. The way he was staring at her, she knew that at last he was scared.

Finally she said, "I'm going to the police. I could go alone, but they would pay more attention if there were two of us."

"What will the police do?"

"They will help us find Hannah. She will know what to do. Daddy will listen to her."

It was his turn not to answer right away. But at last he said one word. "Okay."

They made their plans carefully. They took baths and washed their hair and put out their best clothes for the visit to the police. "It's important to make a good impression," she told Carl. "If we go in looking like bums, they will think it's just an act."

He even helped her clean up the house a little so that the police wouldn't be so shocked.

"We must make them believe Daddy is sick," she kept repeating. "Not that he's drunk. We'll tell them he has some mysterious disease."

"But he doesn't," Carl protested.

"Yes, he does. He's possessed. By something in this house. It got you. It got me for a while."

That night they went to bed early. It had been a long day. They were both exhausted.

It was just growing light when she woke up. A figure in black was standing by her bed. Soft hands were stroking her face, hands like silk. For the first time in days, she felt a sense of happiness. Kathleen smiled up at the woman, but her face was concealed by a heavy veil. But Kathleen knew she loved her. Her perfume made Kathleen's head swim. It was so sweet and delicate. There was nothing in the world she wanted except for the woman to go on stroking her.

When the woman turned away and opened the door, Kathleen felt sick, deserted. But a white hand beckoned to her.

She leaped out of bed.

On the landing, she saw her brother on the floor below. He was sleepwalking, his hands outstretched. The woman in black was right behind him. They were moving toward her father's bedroom door. Kathleen almost sobbed with relief. Everything was going to be all right. They would always be together—she and Carl and her father and this wonderful woman. They would live happily ever after. She followed.

Something brushed against her legs. Startled, she looked down. But it was just the old tom. His back was arched and he was terrified, but he was following. He would not go back, even when she tried to tell him to scat. Then she forgot him.

The woman had opened the door to Kathleen's father's room. The doctor was asleep, sprawled on the bed. She pulled back the sheets and blankets and unbuttoned his pajama jacket. Then she moved a soft finger across his throat, lifting his head with the other hand.

It was then Kathleen saw the knife in her brother's hand, the big old kitchen knife that was so sharp Auntie Boo never let them touch it.

Kathleen ran down the steps screaming, "Carl, wake up!"

He turned around, startled. The knife dropped from his hand. The tomcat let out a yowl. The woman in black reached for the knife. The cat clawed her hand. Then he jumped to her head and tore down the veil.

The creature let out an unearthly squeal. Kathleen and Carl clung together. For the sight was too horrible to take in.

The body and hair and even the neck were those of a beautiful woman. But the face was that of a repulsive animal. Huge jowls of thick blobby fat hung down over the white neck. The nose thickened into a snout. Small, evil eyes blinked above a blubbery, drooling mouth containing two huge ugly yellowing tusks.

Behind them they heard a roar of anger and disbelief. Their father had wakened and seen the creature, too. As the three of them stared, it vanished into the black stone wall. Nothing remained except the knife that had been meant to cut the throat of the doctor. It gleamed up at them from the bare floor.

Suddenly the room started to move. Kathleen lost her balance and Carl fell on top of her. She heard her father's voice: "Children, it's an earthquake! We have to get out!"

He half-pulled, half-pushed them down the stairs. The whole house was rocking back and forth. Kathleen and Carl got outside. Just as they did, the front door came off the hinges and fell on their father's legs. Gasping and grunting, they were finally able to get it off. But he couldn't walk. They dragged him over to the tree, the big oak tree where Auntie Boo had once found Carl after he had walked in his sleep.

They heard an awful sound. The big black boulder that had held up the house tottered and fell, crushing it.

When the doctor got out of the hospital, his broken legs still in splints, he decided to move back to Chicago. With the insurance money, he bought a house on Sheridan Road, not far from us. Auntie Boo came back to run it. And the neighbors, all patients of the doctor, were happy to have him back.

But he was different. He no longer looked like a jolly

Santa Claus. He no longer teased you into forgetting when you had to have a needle for immunization injections. He was still kind and gentle, but sad. Kathleen was a lot different, too. I liked her much better. She no longer tried to boss me around.

Once she told me, "I wish Hannah would come back. We were all mean to her. Auntie Boo says it was the creature that did it. I think it must have been one of those elementals."

"Was it an awful sight?" I asked.

Kathleen shivered. "I could have died on the spot. I guess we almost did."

She told me her father had no idea what had become of Hannah. He had tried every way he could think of to find her. He even thought of hiring a detective; then he realized Hannah might not like that. "She'll get in touch when she wants to," he told the children. "The folks back in Connecticut know where we are."

The months went on. Auntie Boo was having a bad time with her arthritis, and the doctor hired a housekeeper. It wasn't any fun over at the O'Rourkes' anymore. We kids didn't like to go there after school. One night, after a basketball game, Carl walked home with me. He was almost more changed than anybody. Instead of kidding around, he seemed shy. He blurted out to me, "If nobody else is going to try to find Hannah, I will. How does she know we want her back unless we tell her?"

"How are you going to do it?"

"I don't know. It's rough being a little kid."

One night my mother came into my room, where I had

been studying. She sat down. "Can you keep a secret?" When I nodded eagerly—I felt very grown-up, sharing secrets with my mother—she said, "Hannah is back in town. She's been writing to me, and I've invited her to stay in our spare room until—well, I'm hoping she and the doctor will make it up. But don't tell anybody."

Hannah came that night, after I was asleep. And she was still asleep when I went to school. But that noon she was sitting in the kitchen, watching Mother fix soup, when I came home for lunch. She looked different. She was thinner and her hair was fixed a new way. She was wearing a smart suit, the kind my mother wore.

She told me she had been teaching in Cambridge, Massachusetts, and taking courses under a local professor who had once taught at Harvard. Then she turned to my mother. "Shall I tell her what kind of courses?"

Mother smiled and nodded.

"I've been studying witchcraft. You may think this is silly, but the smartest scientists are beginning to believe that witches and ghosts really exist. The professor and I went down to Satan's Kingdom and tried to find out just why it got its name. It seems that back in colonial days, before the colonies broke away from England, there was a beautiful but evil woman who was married to a governor. She did such terrible things that, as an example, he had her tied to a stake with ropes attached to wild horses. They tore her apart. Ever afterward, she was supposed to haunt the place. That's why the natives called it Satan's Kingdom. It was dangerous to go through there, especially on horses. Many people were killed."

"Do you think it was her ghost that did the awful things? The ghost with the pig face? Kathleen says it was an elemental."

Hannah shrugged. "We don't know so many things. It might be. All I know is that I wouldn't live there again for all the tea in China."

"Do you forgive the doctor now?" Mother asked her.

Hannah smiled. "I never hated him. I couldn't. But I didn't understand how such a wonderful, kind man could change so. I believe he was bewitched. I think Carl was bewitched, too. And the evil spirit got rid of Auntie Boo, making her think I was trying to drive her crazy."

Word got around that Hannah was back. It wasn't long before the doctor was at our house every night. And before very long our spare room was empty. She was back with the doctor and the children and Auntie Boo, and the atmosphere in the house was so different, everybody loved going there.

Nobody ever mentioned the pig-faced woman. One day, however, when Carl and I were helping plan a surprise party for Kathleen's fourteenth birthday, I asked Hannah if she still might be around in Satan's Kingdom. Auntie Boo, who was frosting the birthday cake, tried to shush me.

But Hannah said, "She might as well know. We've sold the property and so has the man who raised guard dogs. A group of promoters are building a big condominium for senior citizens. They've changed the name from Satan's Kingdom to Sunset Towers."

"I don't think the creature would bother a place like that," Carl said. "She liked action."

Hannah just smiled. "I guess she could do evil anywhere. Well, thank goodness, that is all behind us."

Chapter 4
THE CHOCOLATE GHOST

What would you do if you found out your house was haunted?

Some folks don't mind, if the ghost happens to be a friendly sort who watches television with the children and doesn't scare the dog.

But mischievous ghosts can get tiresome. Like naughty children, they can go too far. And once in a while, a truly frightening and dangerous ghost comes along. How do you get rid of it?

Often priests or ministers are summoned. But very few modern men of the cloth have had experience with exorcism, getting rid of troublesome spirits. Or the frantic family calls in the police. I'm not sure why. Neither are the police. Because ghosts can't be arrested or given a summons.

If you should have unwelcome ghosts, I advise you to do what I did. I simply looked in the Yellow Pages of the telephone book and found Dr. Stephen Kaplan listed under the heading "Occult Research." I called his number and told him I was writing a book of true ghost stories. He said he knew lots of them. But he was very busy during the day. Could I come to see him at night?

I arranged to meet him the following Tuesday night at his office on Long Island. He said, "It's not easy to find. You'd better get a cab driver who knows his way around."

Tuesday was cold and rainy. It was already dark when I set out. A neighbor asked where I was going and I said, "To see someone who knows all about ghosts and vampires."

She gave me a funny look. "Where?"

"Someplace out on Long Island."

She said, "You'd better tell your super to let me in if you're not back tomorrow morning. I'll take care of your dog."

It was my turn to give her a funny look. I'm a reporter and I live right in the middle of New York City, where people are mugged regularly, and I have never been afraid to go anyplace alone. But ghost experts are something else again.

I said to her, "Listen. The address and telephone number of the man I'm seeing are on my telephone pad. If I don't get back, you can tell the police where I was going."

Steve Kaplan couldn't have been more of a surprise to a nervous reporter. He's a muscular young man with curly hair who looks more like a football player than someone who is on intimate terms with evil creatures. He works and lives in a basement apartment on a quiet, dark street. And he has a secretary and researcher who is equally attractive, a twenty-two-year-old girl named Roxanne.

Steve majored in sociology and was a teacher. Then he began to have strange experiences, psychic experiences. One day he was making a call from a street telephone booth when he floated out of his body. For several minutes, he was up on top of the telephone booth looking down at his body holding the receiver. He told his doctor about it. The doctor suggested he might be having sinus trouble.

Steve decided to look for better reasons. He bought some books on the supernatural. He discovered he had psychic gifts. So now he devotes his full time to that kind of work. He heads a group of psychics who meet regularly to investigate supernatural happenings. He teaches courses in the occult at high schools and colleges. He has helped worried parents find missing children by psychic means. The night I visited him he had a phone call from a girl who had lost her cat. He had Roxanne get him a map of where she lived; he concentrated on it for a while and finally told her the cat was alive and hiding in the basement of a brownstone house across the street. (This was for free.)

And he knows pretty much the habits and haunts of every ghost who has operated on Long Island in the last eight years.

He was called in on the case of the Chocolate Ghost in the summer of 1974. He was successful twice in banishing him. But the ghost was still around in the winter of 1974 and the following summer, Steve believes, and responsible for a terrible murder. And he fears that one of these days it may turn up again with bloody hands to bother innocent people.

In the summer of 1974, Lee and Sally Sloat rented a beach cottage on the ocean. They had just been married and planned to take the summer off before they started new jobs in September.

One morning in July they were sitting on the terrace when they felt a sudden chill. Sally went inside to get a sweater. When she came back, Lee asked, "Are you cooking something? I smell chocolate."

Sally sniffed the air. "I'm not cooking. But I smell chocolate, too. Do you suppose there's an open box of candy around?"

She sat down on the beach chair and jumped up with a little shriek. "Lee, you know I don't like practical jokes."

He stared at her in amazement. "What are you talking about?"

"There was something horrible in that chair. I felt as though I were sitting down in somebody's lap."

He said, "There's nothing there."

"Then I'm losing my mind. Let's go for a swim." She ran down the beach toward the ocean. Lee was behind her. They'd always had the beach to themselves. But today there was a teen-age boy standing in the surf. He wore blue jeans cut off at the knee. He had sandy hair and freckles. He grinned at them and plunged into the ocean. Then he disappeared. They didn't see him swimming. He just disap-

peared. And the smell of chocolate came back strongly, mingling with the salt air.

Lee and Sally stood there, staring out to sea. She was the first to speak. "I think there's something very wrong. Either that boy just drowned or . . ."

"He's a ghost," Lee said. "I opt for that. Let's go in the water."

But they didn't enjoy the swim as much as usual. The ocean seemed unusually cold, even for the North Atlantic. They decided to have lunch.

They were still eating when the woman from the post office came by. A package had just arrived from Sally's mother, and she had decided to drop it off on her way home. Sally invited the postmistress to have some iced tea, and opened the package. It was a chocolate cake. She went inside to get some plates and a knife to cut it.

She saw him standing by the counter. He was dressed just as he'd been down at the beach, except for battered sneakers. She dropped the plates and screamed.

Lee and the postmistress hurried in. The boy vanished. But in his place was a shimmering blue blob, a kind of cloud, that floated over their heads and out to the terrace.

She blurted out, "I saw it again!"

Lee put his arm around her shoulders. "There's some kind of a turtle that's been hanging around the house. Sally doesn't like it. I'll get rid of it this afternoon, I promise you. And I'll sweep up the glass later. Let's get some fresh plates and have that cake. It looks great."

But when they returned to the terrace, the cake was gone. The box was still there, with the brown paper wrappings. But no cake.

After the bewildered postmistress had gone, Sally told Lee, "Don't make any wisecracks. I saw him again. And he took that cake."

"He probably likes chocolate."

"That's not funny. What are you going to do about him?"

"Don't get upset, Sally. He hasn't done any harm."

"Except stealing the cake. And making me drop the plates. I'm scared, Lee. I don't like this place anymore. I wish we hadn't paid for the whole summer."

To calm her, Lee suggested that they go over to East Hampton and take some friends out to dinner that night. They were old friends, and the two couples had a good time. It was near midnight when Lee and Sally drove back to the cottage.

Sally went into the cottage while Lee parked the car. She was in the bedroom taking off her dress when she heard a tap on the window. Thinking it was Lee, she opened it.

The boy stood there, grinning. She pushed down the window. When Lee came in, he noticed the smell of chocolate before she was able to speak. He reached for the telephone and called the estate agent, waking her up.

"We can't take this. We didn't rent a haunted house. You have to get our money back."

The agent's voice was hoarse with sleep. "I'll come around in the morning. If this is your idea of a joke—"

Lee said it was no joke. And Sally was grimmer than he was. She insisted on sleeping on the living-room couch that night, so Lee tried to sleep on a chair opposite her, to keep her company. The next morning they were both tired and cross. And a visit from the agent didn't make them feel any better. At first she laughed at the whole idea of a ghost who smelled like chocolate. But when Lee said that he wanted his money back for the month of August and that they were going to leave, she got serious.

"Listen, young man. I've had these tricks played on me before. You're not going to get your money back, and you're not going to leave me with an unrented cottage in the middle of the season. Ghost or no ghost, you made a bargain."

She slammed the front door when she left. She also slammed the door of her car and roared off.

Lee went to the police. The sergeant was sympathetic, but it was obvious he thought Lee had a timid little wife on his hands who thought she saw spooks.

"There's a family over at Seaford had something called poltergeists—noisy ghosts, that is—a few years back. They got rid of them. You might call and find out what they did."

Polter is from a German word meaning "to make noise" and *geist* is German for "ghost." Lee had heard about them. They would invade a house and break cups and smash bottles. He called the number the sergeant had given him.

The woman was very sympathetic. "We nearly went out of our minds. My poor little boy was a nervous wreck because the police accused him of doing all those nasty tricks. The most encouragement I can give you is that they eventually get tired and go away."

Lee said, "We only have two months. And they won't give us our rent money back. We can't afford to go anyplace else."

"Wait. There's a nice man named Dr. Kaplan who

came to see us after there was all the publicity in the newspaper. He spent one night in the house with us and proved to the police Jimmy wasn't at fault. Do you want his number?"

That was how Steve Kaplan heard about the chocolate ghost.

He offered to hold a séance at the beach cottage on Saturday night, three days away. He explained he needed the time to gather together a group with psychic powers.

"Meanwhile," he said, "don't leave your wife alone if you can help it. He's appeared mostly to her. I think that if there is danger, she is the one most likely to be hurt. Don't tell her this. Just watch her."

The three days seemed endless for Lee and Sally. They went through the house and made sure there was nothing made with chocolate in the kitchen or anyplace else. Yet they smelled it constantly.

"I'm beginning to hate chocolate," Sally told Lee. He nodded. He felt the same way.

But at least the ghost never appeared to them during that time. They even went back to sleeping in the bedroom. Lee was careful to stay with his wife all the time. Being no fool, she caught on.

"It's me he's after, isn't it? Well, I just know one thing. If this Dr. Kaplan can't help us, I can't stay here. This is no vacation. It's like being in a torture chamber."

On Saturday night, Steve Kaplan arrived in a station wagon with six members of his psychic group. They waited to arrive until after sunset, because darkness invites psychic manifestations.

The purpose of a séance is to attract spirits and encourage them to show themselves. All the people who participate are told to keep their minds as blank as possible, concentrating on the candle in the middle of the circle. No other lights are turned on. Holding hands, keeping very still, and trying not to let minds wander are not easy work. You can get very stiff and tired. And all too often, nothing happens. As Steve explained to Lee, it's the same principle as when you go to the dentist with a toothache, all too often it disappears as soon as you enter the office.

However, just the fact that psychics have gathered together, and formed the magic circle, sometimes frightens the ghost away. This is true especially if the ghost is essentially evil. Unhappy ghosts or ghosts with nothing to hide usually welcome attention.

In the séance group that Steve brought was a fourteen-year-old girl named Pamela. As a rule, Steve didn't include teen-agers in his séances. Most of them don't have the patience to concentrate for long periods of time. Pam, however, was exceptional. A pretty girl with very blond hair and huge blue eyes, she was an honor student and a talented actress. She had played many leads in school plays. Steve wanted her because she was about the age the chocolate ghost seemed to be. More important, she had demonstrated her psychic gifts over and over.

She and her twin brother, Phil, a young man who was just as attractive as Pam, were very close. Their divorced mother worked as a television actress in a daytime serial and was gone most of the day. Phil, although he wasn't a bit psychic, almost always came with Pam to the meetings of Steve's group. They took care of each other.

Once she begged him not to go on a canoe trip with some friends. He didn't understand why, but he agreed not to go, to please her. On the trip, the canoe overturned and two boys were drowned.

When he had a bad case of poison ivy, Pam stayed home from school to nurse him. The teacher was giving a test on the day she returned. Pam explained she wasn't prepared, but the teacher told her to do her best.

While Pam was struggling, the teacher—who, like many others, thought Pam was special—came and stood by her. She didn't say anything, just put a comforting hand on her shoulder. A kind of screen, like a television, appeared in front of Pam's eyes, with the answers to the questions that had been bothering her.

Afterward, she told the teacher, "I think I read your mind."

When he asked Pam to attend the séance, Steve had assured Phil he and Roxanne would pick her up and bring her home. "I have a feeling she'll be useful," he said.

She was.

He decided to hold the séance in the living room of the beach cottage, near both the kitchen and the terrace where the ghost had appeared. All the lights were turned out. Only the candle in the middle of the circle was lighted. Because metal interferes with psychic appearances, the women were asked to remove their jewelry and the men took off their watches and emptied their pockets of change and keys.

An hour passed and nothing happened. Steve called for a break so the people in the circle could stand up and move around, get circulation back. Pam disappeared for a minute. When she came back, she had a chocolate bar in her hands.

"I brought it along and left it in the car. I thought maybe the ghost might take it as a friendly gesture."

Steve agreed. He put the bar close to the candle. When they went back into the magic circle, things began to happen right away. First there was a cold breeze. The candle flickered. Then a mist, like a cloud with sun behind it, formed over the heads of the group. There was a smell of chocolate so strong it was almost overpowering. Slowly, the chocolate bar floated up and was sucked into the cloud.

Then there was a change. Some of the group saw the vapor form into the shape of a person without features. Some only saw a series of circles. Steve saw the boy in blue jeans. So did Pam.

Sally, who was not in the circle, screamed. It was the eeriest sound imaginable. When Steve replayed it later on his tape recorder, it didn't sound as though it had come from a human throat.

Sally began to gasp. "I can't get my breath. Something is choking me. Help, please!"

Steve broke the circle and he and Lee dragged Sally out onto the terrace. In a few minutes she was all right. In fact, she began to apologize. "It seems ridiculous to have been so frightened with all of you around. But I'm terrified of the ghost. I'm sure he wants to kill me."

A silent, exhausted group drove home from the beach cottage. When Steve took Pam up to her door, she had a wan smile for him. "Well, the chocolate bar worked, didn't it?"

The next day, Roxanne drove out to the beach to find out what she could. Nobody had ever seen or heard about a chocolate ghost. Then she found a blind man who acted as caretaker for the houses the summer people closed up when they left for the winter.

He told her, "I wouldn't see him, of course. But many's the time I've gone into a place that was all boarded up and I smelled chocolate. Is he dangerous?"

Roxanne said, honestly, that she didn't know. But she warned him to be careful. She went back to report to Steve. He had good news.

Sally and Lee had telephoned him to thank him. Sally had said, "Right after you left last night, I had the most wonderful feeling of relief. I know the ghost is gone. The whole cottage feels different. The sun is warmer. Thank everybody who came out to help us."

At the next meeting of his psychic group, Steve made a report of the case and played the tape. Afterward, Phil and Pam came and asked him if they could have a word in private.

Outside, Phil said, "Pam doesn't want the rest to know. But I insisted that she tell you. The chocolate ghost is at our house."

Steve groaned. "Well, we'll just have to hold another séance and try to make him go away."

Pam shook her bright head. "No. I don't mind having him around. He's company."

"Pam, he's dangerous."

Pam laughed. "Don't worry. He won't hurt me. He likes me."

Behind her, Phil made a face. Steve said, "Pam, you

don't realize what might happen. I'm sure he tried to choke Sally."

Pam set her jaw stubbornly. "He won't hurt me. I know. Otherwise, I would never have invited him to come to my house."

"When did you do that?"

"At the séance, silly. I just concentrated hard, telling him if he was ready to come and live with Phil and me, he should pick up the chocolate bar. And he did."

"Does your mother know?"

She shook her head. "She's in a state. She's afraid they may write her out of the television show. He'll never bother her, anyway."

"Are you sure?"

"Of course. He promised. And I promised him I wouldn't tell her or send him away. Don't you trust me?"

"Yes. But I don't trust him."

"Steve, don't interfere. I know what I'm doing."

Steve wasn't satisfied. After all, gifted psychic or not, she was just a teen-ager. But other things came up and he was too busy to worry about Pam.

Then one morning, when he was still having his coffee, the doorbell rang.

Phil stood there. "I have to see you. It's about the ghost."

Steve asked him to come in and offered him coffee. Phil shook his head. "I'm in training. Could I have a glass of milk?"

He sat down opposite Steve with his milk and absentmindedly helped himself to toast. "Pam has a crush on the ghost. Never before has she had time for boys or dating.

But now—well, she's nuts about him. She keeps baking him chocolate cakes."

"Can you see him?"

"No. She says that's because I resent him. But I know when he's around because she acts so goofy. I'm scared, Steve. I don't know why, but I am. Pam is bright. But she's so—so trusting."

Steve said, "I'm scared, too. We have to get rid of him."

"I thought of putting rat poison in one of the cakes. But what if Pam ate a piece? Or my mother?"

Steve said, "That wouldn't work. The ghost won't leave so long as he feels she wants him there. Phil, who's the most popular boy around? I mean, both with the fellows and the girls? Someone a little older than you and Pam."

Phil ate another piece of toast. "There's Johnny Lester. He's a lifeguard at the beach. He's going to UCLA in the fall. The girls all think he's fantastic."

"If you asked him to do something for you, would he?"

"I suppose so. He's a nice guy. We talk sports a lot."

"Ask him to date Pam a couple of times. Say you want to take her mind off a fellow you don't like. Don't tell him it's a ghost. Would he?"

Phil said, "It's worth trying. He has a sister. And he told me once he thought Pam was great."

He took the last piece of toast and left.

Neither Pam nor Phil came to the psychic meeting that week—or the next. In late August, Steve suggested to Roxanne that they might drop by the house and find out what was going on.

Pam opened the door. She was wearing a frilly dress, instead of her usual jeans, and her hair was cut a new way.

She apologized when she saw them. "I know you wonder why I haven't been to meetings. But Johnny has been talking to me about my career. They have a wonderful drama department at UCLA. He thinks maybe I could get a scholarship when I graduate."

Johnny came to the door. He was a tall, slim boy with a nice smile. "I'm sorry to be taking up so much of Pam's time. But I'm leaving for California pretty soon and I won't be back until Christmas vacation. We have a lot of plans to make."

Roxanne drew Pam aside. "What happened to the chocolate ghost?"

Pam shrugged. "I guess he's gone someplace else. He really got to be a nuisance. Always hanging around when I wanted to see someone else."

"Did he ever try to hurt you?"

"Of course not. I wasn't afraid of him. But a real boyfriend is much more satisfactory than a ghost. Don't you agree?"

Roxanne and Steve left the young couple to their plans. As he closed the file on the chocolate ghost that night, Steve remarked, "I hope we've heard the last of him."

But they hadn't.

Sally and Lee didn't return to the beach cottage that next summer. It was rented to a single woman who came out alone from New York on weekends. She made no attempt to be friendly. The local people would see her arrive on Friday night and unpack a box of groceries from her car. Sometimes she'd be sunning on the terrace when they went

by on the beach. But she was always alone—apparently by choice.

One weekend they saw her arrive. But she did not leave as usual on Monday, although there were no signs of life in the house. By the middle of the week, the people next door decided to tell the police.

The sergeant broke in. The poor woman had had her neck broken and was stretched out on her bed, a twisted horror. Nothing else had been disturbed. The verdict was murder by an unknown person. The search was complicated by the fact that they could find no fingerprints, and nothing was missing from her closets or her pocketbook.

The sergeant had his own ideas, which he kept to himself. He wasn't going to risk being made a laughing-stock. But he told Steve about it later. When he discovered the body, mingled with the hideous smell of death was the even more sickening aroma of chocolate.

Chapter 5

WHINEY THE MONSTER

Last spring a cousin in Minneapolis wrote and said a friend of theirs was coming to New York and wanted to go to the circus. Would I get tickets and go with him?

To my surprise, the friend was not a kid but a middle-aged man with a string of drugstores.

He had more fun than the kids. He laughed at the clowns and shuddered at the high-wire acts and loved the tigers and elephants. But when the performing monkeys came out, he was suddenly quiet.

One particular monkey, about the height of a six-year-old child, fascinated him. It wore a yellow vest and green pants and skipped with a rope and rode a bike and roller-skated.

My cousin's friend, whom I shall call Arthur, said to me, "I once had a monkey like that. His name was Whiney."

Later he told me the strange story of Whiney, who turned into a monster. He said I could use it in this book if I changed his name.

"Because," he said, "I still feel guilty about old Whiney."

Arthur was an only child. His father, a silent Swede and a lumberjack, was fifty years old before he got married. He brought his young wife from Minneapolis to a log cabin in the woods of northern Minnesota. They lived on a lake so small it wasn't on any of the maps. There were no other people for miles.

It never occurred to him that his wife and little boy might be lonely. Arthur's mother worked hard, cooking, making all their clothes, rising early and going to bed with the chickens.

As soon as Arthur was old enough, he had chores, too. He fed the chickens and collected the eggs. Once he had a pet hen who answered to her name, Becky. His father stopped that.

"We raise chickens for food, son."

On Saturday, Arthur's father drove his family in the buggy to Thieves' Junction, fifteen miles away. There they sold eggs and chickens to the general store and brought back kerosene and cloth and bags of feed.

One Saturday there was a street fair in Thieves' Junction. Arthur fell in love with a mangy old monkey who was dressed up like a boy and could do tricks like turning cartwheels.

He begged his father to buy the monkey for him. Arthur's father laughed. "That smelly thing? I wouldn't have him around."

So Arthur invented his own monkey. He was just Arthur's size and his name was Whiney. Not only could he turn cartwheels, he could do everything Arthur could do, including talk. He lived in the lake, underneath the dock.

Whenever Arthur did something naughty, and was scolded, he would always say, "Whiney did it."

Finally Arthur's father lost his patience. He hated whining kids. And he hated Arthur's way of blaming things on a monkey that didn't exist.

One day he told Arthur, "Son, you are five years old. You should know right from wrong. And it's wrong to blame a creature who doesn't exist, when you are bad."

"But Whiney is real. He's my friend."

"Don't lie to your father."

"I'm not lying. Whiney is real, and I love him more than anyone in the world. More than I do you!"

Arthur's father gave him the worst spanking Arthur had ever had. Afterward, Arthur's mother came into Arthur's room where he lay on the bed sobbing. "That was a terrible thing you said to your father. You must ask him to forgive you."

"He told me Whiney wasn't real. He is. He's my best friend. He loves me and I love him."

"More than you do me?"

"No. It's different. He has time to play with me. You're always working."

"Arthur, please. Forget Whiney."

Arthur shook his head.

"Darling, you must. Or your father will be angry with us both. I tell you what I'll do. If you forget Whiney, or tell him to go away, I'll invite your Aunt Irma to come for a visit and bring your cousin Ralph with her. He's just your age. Then you'll have a real playmate."

"Whiney is real."

"Then you must tell him to go away. Promise me."

Arthur finally promised. The next day, he told Whiney what had happened. Whiney was very angry. He ran in the henhouse and threw the nests around and smashed the eggs and frightened the chickens. Then he ran off toward the lake, saying, "You'll be sorry. I'll get even. Just wait."

Arthur didn't tell his father what Whiney had done. He took the blame himself. His father didn't scold him. He said, "You're man enough to take the blame yourself. For once." And when they went to town on Saturday, he bought Arthur an unexpected treat, an ice cream cone.

Arthur missed Whiney. But he enjoyed the cone—and his father's approval.

That night, someone tapped at Arthur's bedroom window. He woke up. Whiney was looking at him through the pane. Only he had changed. He had grown tall enough to look in the window, tall as a big bear. His nice brown fur had turned a horrible shade of green and was covered with slime. And his big teeth were green with moss.

"Open the window. I want to talk to you."

Arthur got out of bed and opened the window a little crack, not big enough for Whiney to get in. "You have to go away. My father says so. My cousin Ralph is coming to visit, so I don't need you anymore."

Whiney howled. The sound made Arthur's hair stand on end. He ran and jumped back into bed. Hundreds of little lizards ran out of Whiney's mouth and crawled across the window sill into Arthur's room. Then they scrambled onto Arthur's bed and started biting him.

Arthur screamed for his mother.

She said, "It was just a dream. You don't need to feel guilty about sending Whiney away. He wasn't real."

Arthur shook his head. "He was real. So were the lizards. They bit me."

His mother unbuttoned his jacket. Sure enough, there were red spots all over his arms and body.

"I think it's chicken pox," she told Arthur's father. "I'll keep him in bed a couple of days."

But as the day wore on, Arthur got worse. His small body twisted in convulsions. In the middle of the night, they hitched up the wagon and bundled up Arthur and drove him to the doctor in Thieves' Junction.

He was very sick for many weeks. When he got well, his Aunt Irma and his cousin Ralph came for a visit. And when they returned to Minneapolis in September, Arthur went with them. It was decided he would live with Aunt Irma and go to school in Minneapolis.

Arthur hated to leave his mother. She finally had to tell him his father was very ill and she had to stay and nurse him. But she promised to send for Arthur when his dad got better.

His father died the following spring. Arthur's mother moved down to Minneapolis and they lived in a sprawling gabled house with Aunt Irma and Uncle Jim and Arthur's cousins. It was a big, lively household. Arthur tried to feel sad about his father. But his new life was very exciting. He had lots of boys and girls to play with. One particular little girl was his special friend. Her name was Mary Louise, and her father owned a drugstore. Arthur used to go there after school with her, and Mary Louise's dad would treat them to sodas.

Sometimes in the summer, Uncle Jim would fill the station wagon with kids and drive up to the cabin in the woods. He bought a rowboat and taught Arthur how to fish. But Arthur was always glad to get back to Minneapolis. He felt as though Whiney were still around, watching him. It was silly, he supposed. But Whiney still seemed very real.

When he was ten, he got a paper route and a job in the local grocery store. He worked after school and all day Saturday delivering orders. He gave the money to his mother to save for his university education. When summer came, the grocer hired Arthur full-time, he was such a good worker. So he didn't have time to go to the camp anymore. His cousins still enjoyed it, but Arthur wanted to go to the university with Mary Louise.

When that time came, Mary Louise's father urged him to become a pharmacist, saying that when he graduated he would give him a job. Arthur got the job, and he and Mary Louise were married the following fall.

Arthur did so well his father-in-law bought a second store and put him in charge. He and Mary Louise bought a nice house on Colfax Avenue with a big yard for kids. Mike was born, then Bobby, and four years later, Dora.

Arthur's mother died when Mike was eleven and Bobby was ten. She left the cabin in the woods to Arthur. Nobody had been up there for a couple of years. And Arthur hadn't been there since Mike was born. He always said he was too busy.

Mary Louise suggested that he take the children up when school closed in June and see what shape the place was in. If it was still livable, she said, they might consider fixing it up as a summer home.

The children were excited about a camping trip. Arthur got out a shotgun that had belonged to his father and oiled it and bought some ammunition, telling the kids he might bag a rabbit. He packed fishing rods, and the kids took their sleeping bags. Mary Louise gave them enough groceries for a week.

"Don't hurry back," she told Arthur. "I'll help out in the store. You need a good rest."

The trip didn't seem as long as when Arthur was a little boy. It was dusk when they got there, a beautiful night. The moon was almost full and the lake looked peaceful. An old rowboat Uncle Jim had bought was up on the dock. The children put it in the water while Arthur looked around the house and filled the kerosene lamps. He made coffee on an old iron stove, and the children roasted hot dogs around the open fire in the living room.

He went to bed early, in the room his parents had used. Dora crawled into her sleeping bag—the children were all in his old room—but the boys wanted to stay up for a while. Arthur agreed. After all, it was a vacation.

"Just lock the cabin door when you come in," he said. "There might be tramps around."

The boys put on jackets and sat out on the dock. The air had a nip in it, and around nine o'clock a mist came up on the water. Mike shivered. "I'm for bed. Let's see if we can catch a fish before breakfast."

Bobby stood up, too. Then he said, "Wait a minute. What's that?"

Something was coming out of the mist from underneath the pier. For a minute, they thought it was a man. Then they realized it was some kind of animal. It walked on its hind legs, but its arms were very long. It reached the shore and waded out of the water. In the moonlight, they could see that it was covered with something that looked like matted weeds. It dropped to all fours and ran around behind the cabin.

"It looks like a gorilla," Bobby said.

"In a lake in Minnesota?" Mike laughed scornfully. "Gorillas live in jungles, stupid. It's probably some big old bear. Let's turn in. I want fish for breakfast."

The next day was so beautiful even Bobby forgot all about the strange animal. Both boys caught fish and their father fried them for breakfast. Afterward they tramped through the woods.

In the afternoon it was warm enough so they could all go swimming. Arthur enjoyed it as much as the kids. He spent a long time teaching Dora to dive off the pier. The water was cold, but the sun was warm.

Arthur made chili for dinner. As they were sitting down, he said, "I'm hungry as a bear."

That reminded the boys about the animal they had

seen last night. They didn't like to scare Dora, so Mike simply asked his father if there were bears around.

His father shook his head. "I shouldn't think so. I've never heard of any in this area."

"Bob and I saw some kind of an animal coming out of the water last night."

Arthur put down his fork. "What did it look like?"

"It was covered with green slime. Bob said it looked like a gorilla. But not in this climate. And gorillas don't like water, do they? Cold water, anyway."

Arthur said, "Look, kids, it's got to be a bear. They're not dangerous if you don't annoy them. But, you know, I think I caught cold this afternoon. I was hungry, but now food just doesn't appeal to me. I'll take a couple of aspirin and go to bed. You clean up, will you?"

After Dora had gone, reluctantly, to bed, the boys decided to go out on the dock again. The moon was full. This time there was no mist. They waited silently. After a long time, Mike said, "That's it!"

In the distance, a creature was swimming. Its powerful arms were pushing the body through the water. And it was headed toward the dock.

"Let's see if Dad's awake," Bob suggested.

Their father was awake, but his face seemed red and swollen. "I've got a bug, I'm afraid. Don't get near me. I feel awful. I think I'd better take an antibiotic. There're some pills in my suitcase, if you'd get them and a glass of water."

Bobby went for the water while Mike found the pills. "Dad, we saw the thing again. It was swimming."

Arthur jerked upright. He was staring out of the window. Mike turned. A huge head was looking at them, a head that in a horrible way seemed almost human. Slimy green hair hung down over the face. Evil eyes glinted at them. But the most awful thing was the mouth, with its huge black tongue and its scummy teeth.

Arthur said, "Mike, the gun is on the chest in the living room. There's a box of shells beside it. Bring them here."

Mike arrived with the gun at the same time Bobby came with the glass of water. Arthur loaded the gun. He got out of bed. "Stand back, boys." The corners of the creature's awful mouth lifted in a grin. Arthur dropped the gun's muzzle and unloaded it. The hideous mouth still grinned at them. "I can't do it, boys. I wish I was able to drive. But I'll take the antibiotic and maybe in the morning—"

Mike took the gun from his father's hand. "Dad, what is it?"

"It's Whiney." As he said the word, the creature vanished. Mike ran to the window. It was loping on all fours toward the water.

"What do you mean, Dad?"

"Boys, it's a long story. When I was no bigger than Dora, I had an imaginary playmate, the ways kids do sometimes. He was a monkey named Whiney. My father made me tell him to go away. So he turned into a monster. He lives in the lake, under the dock."

"Is he dangerous, Dad?"

"I don't think so. We'll leave tomorrow. Lock the doors and windows."

After they had locked up, Mike and Bobby got into their sleeping bags. But neither of them slept very much.

They got up early and went out into the kitchen. They decided to let Dora and their father sleep until breakfast was ready. While Bobby cooked bacon, Mike began packing up the rest of the food.

Dora came out and asked what was going on. "We're leaving right after breakfast," Mike told her.

"I think that's mean. I want to go swimming."

"Dad's sick. We've got to get home."

"That isn't fair. I planned to go swimming this morning." Mike told her, shortly, to stop it.

"Go on in the bedroom and start packing."

She left the kitchen, with a sulky pout on her face.

When they took in a plate of bacon and eggs to their father, he shook his head. "I can't swallow. And I'm afraid I can't drive. Mike, after breakfast, you had better take the car and drive to Thieves' Junction and get a doctor. I know you don't have a license yet, but it can't be helped. This is an emergency."

Bobby and Mike ate hastily. They decided Mike had better call their mother from the village. Mike went in to get his father's wallet. Arthur was sleeping.

Bobby said, "I'll stay here with Dora. By the way, where is she?"

They looked in the bedroom. Dora wasn't there. They ran out into the living room. The front door was open and they saw Dora out on the dock, in her bathing suit. As they watched, she dove in.

She was a good little swimmer. And she had no fear of the water. She was swimming out toward where they had seen the monster.

Mike ran for the rowboat. He called to Dora, but she

did not hear him. He started after her. She swam faster, thinking it was a game.

He reached down and pulled her out of the lake. "Just shut up and do what I tell you," he said. He glanced back. Bobby was standing on the dock. Mike waved and Bobby waved back. Mike started rowing back to shore, with Dora grouchily complaining in the seat in front of him.

Suddenly the boat started to rock. Dora screamed. Mike looked down. Two huge black hands were on either side of the boat. The creature was underneath it. With all his clothes on, Bobby jumped in and started swimming toward the boat.

Mike screamed at him, "It's no use. Save yourself." But Bobby paid no attention. The monster let go of the boat and started toward Bobby. Mike handed an oar to Dora. "Hang on tight." Then he grabbed the other oar and stood up, lifting the oar high above his head.

He hit the monster. It went under. Mike reached out and grabbed Bobby. Using the oars like paddles, he and Bobby raced toward the dock. With Mike holding Dora, they jumped to safety, letting the boat drift away. As they watched, Whiney grabbed it, turned it upside down, and jumped up on it. Riding it like a surfboard, he headed toward the dock, his huge arms making circles in the water.

They ran in and locked the door.

Mike looked at his brother. "What are we going to do?"

Bobby said, his voice trembling, "Maybe I can lure him away while you run and get in the car."

"That's a great idea. Drive away and let him kill you."

"Where is he now?"

The three of them looked out the window. Whiney was standing in shallow water. He had turned the boat over and was trying to bail water out of it with his big hands.

Dora said, "We could take him a can and show him how to do it."

Mike laughed. And Dora shook her head. "I'm not being funny. I don't think he's mean. I think he wants to play."

"Play! Don't be a jerk!"

Bobby said slowly, "I think Dora has something. He used to play with Dad when Dad was a little boy. Out there in the water, he could have killed us all if he'd wanted to. I think he's lonesome."

"Okay, wise guy. And where does that leave us? Going out there with a ball and bat and teaching him to hit right-handed curves? You guys are nuts." Mike turned away from the window.

"No, Mike. But I have an idea. Dora and I will go out and help him bail out the boat. Then I'll show him how to row. Meanwhile, you go and get in the car and get the doctor to help Dad."

"And leave you two alone with him? What kind of a brother do you think I am?"

Finally Bobby said, "All three of us will go and talk to him. We'll explain the whole thing. Why Dad had to send him away. How grownups don't understand monsters. That's why he has to stop bothering Dad."

"How is that going to make him feel less lonesome?" Dora put her hand on Mike's arm. "He makes me feel sad. I like him. I really do."

"Well, in that case, we'll invite him to come back to

live with us on Colfax Avenue. He can sleep in your room, Dora. Under the bed. Mom will be crazy about that. Grow up, Dora." Mike stared at his sister impatiently.

Dora said doubtfully, "I guess he would have to brush his teeth and have his hair cut."

"Then he wouldn't be a monster anymore. He'd be a tame old pussycat monkey," Bobby said. "Look, Mike, I have a kind of idea. He's lonesome up here with nobody to play with. Why don't we tell him to come down to Minneapolis and live in Lake Minnetonka? It's a nice big lake and there are lots of people around, plenty of kids. He could be a sensation. Like that monster in Scotland. They would run stories in the newspapers; he'd be a big tourist attraction. Maybe we'd even get our pictures in the paper because we discovered him."

Mike smiled tolerantly. "And I was telling Dora to grow up. You're out of your skull, Bobby."

"It's worth a try," Bobby insisted. "Unless you think of something better. There he is now, looking for us. I think he's smiling."

He was right. Whiney was looking toward the cabin, showing his slimy teeth in what passed for a smile.

"I'm going to teach him how to bail," Dora said. "If you two are afraid, just stay in the cabin."

But Mike insisted on leading the way. And he was the one who taught Whiney how to bail. Afterward he got in the boat and showed him how to use the oars. Then Bobby and Dora came and sat on the dock and Bobby explained the whole situation. He told Whiney how to get to Lake Minnetonka. He assured him it wasn't far from where they lived, and they would come to see him often.

"And you'll be famous. We'll be proud that we were the ones who got you started."

Whiney looked a little stunned. After all these years of living under a dock, it was hard to understand everything they were talking about. He'd even forgotten how to talk. All he could do was grunt. But it was exciting just listening to the three of them.

After a while, he got out of the boat and came and stood by the dock. He smelled awful. Insects buzzed about his slimy fur. After a while, Mike said he had to go and get a doctor for his father and would Whiney please go back and hide for a while.

"Grownups are pretty uptight about monsters," he explained. "It will be different after you're famous. But now, just for a while—"

Whiney rose to the challenge like an old trooper. He kept out of the way when the doctor came. And next day, when Arthur said he felt well enough to drive home, the monster kept his distance. He watched them pack the car and close up the house.

Just before they left, Bobby went out to the dock to say good-bye. Tears ran down the monster's face: horrid globs of thick slime.

"We'll see you this summer in Lake Minnetonka," Bobby said.

Whiney nodded. He grunted several times, and Bobby knew he was trying to say something. But Mike was calling impatiently from the car, telling Bobby they had to get going. Bobby raised one hand. "We'll be seeing you soon," he said.

"And did he come to Lake Minnetonka?" I asked Arthur. We were standing on the corner of Seventh Avenue and Thirty-third Street, after the circus.

Arthur shook his head. "Maybe he got lost. Or maybe somebody hurt him. Anyway, he's not at the camp. We go up there a lot in the summer."

"You're sure he isn't around?"

Arthur shook his head. "No. And in a funny way, we miss him. Maybe it's a good miss. Just the same, I feel guilty."

Then he hailed a cab and went back to his hotel. And I came back home to write down the story he'd told me.

Chapter 6
THE MOST EVIL OF ALL CREATURES

Would you live in a house where somebody had been murdered?

I wouldn't, if I could help it.

Because people who have been murdered, or who have been connected with terrible crimes when living, are earthbound. Their spirits cannot go on to another plane. So they become vampires, the most evil of all creatures.

There are two kinds of vampires.

Dracula, whose ruined castle can still be visited in Romania, was the type who drank blood. He turned himself into a bat by night and flew into the windows of his victims, biting their throats and sucking enough blood so he could exist for another day. Countess Elizabeth Báthory of Hungary bathed in the blood of the women she murdered, in order to stay young.

The second kind are more dangerous and, unfortunately, more common. They are psychic vampires, ghosts who live on in houses where crimes have been committed. They wait for some likely victim to move into the house. Then they attack, sapping the life energy of that person, slowly at first. Soon the victim becomes weaker and weaker. Then, when he or she dies, the vampire takes over the body.

"The nice girl who lives next door or the friendly old man at the supermarket may be a vampire," warns Dr. Stephen Kaplan, who heads the Vampire Research Center of America. Steve, whom you met in the story of the chocolate ghost, says that one of the great problems in avoiding the traps of these evil psychic vampires is that owners and rental agents don't tell prospective buyers or renters that the person who lived in the house was murdered.

Landlords are required by law to do repairs after a murder, replace a stained floor or cover up bloodstains with layers of paint. But they are not compelled to tell you the history of a house or an apartment. So you don't find out until it is too late.

In the following case history of a murder house, it was simply a matter of luck that Steve Kaplan was called in before the vampire could take over.

It was close to midnight on a Friday night when Steve's telephone rang. Ghost investigators, like doctors, can't expect to keep regular hours. Just the same, it had been a hard week and he was asleep.

A woman identified herself as Mrs. Reese. She spoke English with a faint accent. "Our doctor advised us to call you, Dr. Kaplan. He—we seem to have a problem with a ghost. It's hard to believe in this day and age but . . ."

When Steve asked for more information, she said, "Promise me you won't think I'm just a crazy woman. I'd better tell you the whole story."

And the tale she told would have sounded incredible to anyone but a ghost expert like Steve.

The Reeses had been members of an Amish colony, a strict religious sect. Mr. Reese wanted to get away from the old-fashioned atmosphere. He was able to get a job managing a duck farm on Long Island.

The farmer who hired him suggested that he might be able to rent what he referred to as "the old Miller place," some miles away, very cheap. It had been vacant for some time. Local kids said it was haunted.

"But you aren't superstitious, are you?"

Mr. Reese said he definitely wasn't. "We don't believe in ghosts."

"Then go see the rental agent and tell him I sent you. Offer him a couple of months' rent in advance and I'm sure he'll give you a bargain."

The house was in the woods, on a dirt road. It was lonesome. On the other hand, the previous owners had left most of their furniture. Mr. Reese was going to be able to move in with his wife and daughter with only a few possessions, which he could carry in his pickup truck. He made a deal and paid three months' rent in advance. It took most of their savings. The farmer gave him a television set, so Mrs. Reese and their twelve-year-old daughter wouldn't feel lonesome. He also offered them a white shepherd-type farm dog named Blizzard for protection.

At first, Mrs. Reese was so busy it didn't occur to her to be lonesome. She gave the old house a thorough cleaning from top to bottom, with her daughter helping her. Betty was a pretty child, with long, fair curls and blue eyes. She'd never had a television set before, and she loved the big dog. Although he was allowed only in the kitchen of the house, he followed her everywhere outside and they took long walks in the woods.

It was January. Betty's school wouldn't start until February, so they decided she would just study at home for a few weeks. She was a good student, and her father had at one time taught English and mathematics in the Amish school.

But things began to go wrong. Little things, at first.

No matter how much she scoured, Mrs. Reese couldn't get a musty smell out of the cellar. So her husband put up a shelf in the kitchen for her to store the jams and jellies she had brought from Pennsylvania. But the jars kept falling off the shelf and breaking during the night.

Mr. Reese suspected rats, but he mentioned field mice to his wife. He carefully plugged up holes where the animals might come in. But that didn't stop the intruders.

One day, when he was reading his newspaper in the kitchen after dinner, he heard a truck starting up outside. He looked out. His pickup truck was going around the circular driveway. He ran out. There was no one in the driver's seat. He stopped the truck, figuring that some kid might have started it as a joke. But it was no joke to him. The truck had cost money.

When he came in, he was angry. Betty had gone for a walk with Blizzard after dinner. "Do you think she did it?" he asked his wife.

She protested that Betty wouldn't do a thing like that. He calmed down. But that night, when he heard her lessons, Betty wasn't her usual attentive self. She wasn't sorry when he pointed out mistakes. When he was correcting her mathematics paper, she fell asleep.

"She's growing pretty fast," he told his wife. "Maybe she needs a tonic."

That Saturday they took her to the clinic in the next town. The doctor examined Betty carefully and told her parents that, so far as he could tell, she was in excellent health except for slight anemia. He gave them a bottle of medicine.

During the night, the bottle fell off the shelf. In the morning, Betty's mother accused her of breaking it deliberately. Betty denied being downstairs.

"I'm afraid she isn't telling the truth," her mother told her father. "I've been noticing that other things are being chipped and broken. I suspect she has just been going through some phase of naughtiness."

Her father suggested she might be lonesome without anyone to play with except the dog. "She'll be all right when she starts school." At noon he went and got some more medicine from the doctor. He told him he was worried about Betty.

"She's always been so good and obedient. I'm afraid she's—well, my wife thinks it may be some phase."

The young doctor agreed. "She's been raised in a very strict atmosphere. Now that she has more freedom, she may just be seeing how far she can go."

"Well, she won't get away with much more," Mr. Reese assured him. "My wife is a patient woman, but she doesn't approve of unruly children."

He brought home the new bottle of medicine. Betty took some before dinner and threw up. Her mother sent her to bed. "She's been acting strange all day. I was polishing the dining-room table and a cup sailed by me and just missed hitting me in the head. It smashed against the wall. She insisted that she hadn't touched it, that the cup flew of its own accord. A likely story."

The next morning, when Mrs. Reese went in to wake her daughter, she saw a frightful sight. Betty, being young for her age, had always slept with her dolls lined up under the covers with her in bed. But the dolls were in the middle of the floor with their heads torn off.

Betty's mother spanked her. She went downstairs to tell her husband.

"I'm at my wit's end. I don't know what to do. She's like a different child. The doctor said she wasn't sick. So she must be punished. She didn't even cry when I spanked her."

They decided to make her stay in bed all day. One of Betty's great pleasures was tramping through the woods with Blizzard. Betty didn't complain. She just lay in bed, staring at the ceiling. At noon her mother began to worry about her. She took her up some milk toast. Betty said she wasn't hungry. Mrs. Reese gathered up the dolls and their heads and took them downstairs. During the afternoon,

she mended them. Each doll had a name and a history. Betty, who had few toys, had been very attached to them all. Her mother couldn't imagine what had affected the child, to treat them so brutally.

She fixed a special dinner. Just before it was time for Mr. Reese to come home, she went up to her daughter's room with the dolls. She pulled up a chair by the bed and sat down.

"Betty, you know we love you very much. We don't understand why you have to be so naughty at times. Tell me what is wrong."

Betty glanced at the dolls and tears came into her eyes. Her usually rosy cheeks were pale. "Mamma, I'm scared."

"Scared of what?"

"There's a girl who hates me. She comes in the night and pulls my hair. She's the one who hurt my dolls. I'm afraid she's going to hurt me like that."

"Betty, you're imagining things."

"No, I'm not."

"Have you seen her?"

"Of course. She has long, black hair and awful yellow eyes. She wants me to die so she can be your little girl."

"Oh, dearest. Get dressed and come down to dinner. Lying up here all alone, you made up crazy things."

But when Mrs. Reese went into her own bedroom to change from work clothes into a cotton dress for dinner, she found a mess. Everything had been pulled off the hangers and her clothes were in a heap on the floor. And there were footprints all around the walls. It looked as though black shoe polish had been applied to the sole of one of

Betty's slippers and then the slipper had been pressed against the wall, over and over.

She went back to her daughter's room. "I want you to tell me the truth, Betty. I promise not to spank you. Did you mess up my room?"

Betty shook her head.

"Then who did?"

"Blizzard?"

"Blizzard was down in the kitchen with me all afternoon. You were the only one upstairs."

Betty shuddered. "Then it was the girl."

"Betty, don't lie to me."

Betty began to pound on the wall over the bed. When her mother tried to pull her down, her small body stiffened. Then, abruptly, she collapsed, sobbing. "I'm not lying. You won't believe me. It must be true what she said."

"What did she say?"

"That I wasn't your real child, that she was. That was why she had come to take my place."

Mrs. Reese was angry. Betty had been adopted after Mrs. Reese had lost a baby and discovered she couldn't have any more of her own. But from the time Betty was a baby, they had told her she was especially precious to them because they had chosen her. Always before, she had accepted this explanation.

When her husband got home, he suggested that they call the doctor. He was just leaving for his own home when they caught him.

"I'm sorry, I really am. But I can't handle situations such as you describe. I'm just a general practitioner. You need a psychiatrist."

Mr. Reese said, "Then you think she really believes she sees a ghost?"

Silence. Then he added, "But what if there is a ghost? What if the house is haunted?"

"In that case, call a friend of mine called Steve Kaplan. He specializes in haunted houses. I'll give you his number."

"We won't use it," Mr. Reese said firmly. But he took down the number.

That night, Betty's father changed his mind about calling Steve. He and his wife were in bed when they heard Betty scream.

They rushed out and found Betty collapsed in the hall. She couldn't talk for a while. Finally she was able to tell them that she'd wakened with a stomach ache and gone to the bathroom. She hadn't turned on the light because she didn't want to disturb her parents.

In the bathroom, something icy-cold had wrapped itself around her. She couldn't get her breath. It had let go when Betty's parents had turned on the light. But she still couldn't stand up. Her legs were too weak.

Betty's parents looked at each other. Downstairs, Blizzard was howling. It was an unearthly sound.

Mr. Reese's voice broke. "They told me the house was haunted. I didn't believe it. I think we'd better call that man Kaplan."

After listening to the story, Steve asked where the dog slept. When he found out Blizzard was shut in the kitchen, he said, "Give him the run of the house. He'll give you warning if the ghost comes back. And I'll come over tomorrow about dusk."

Anyone who deals with the supernatural gets crank

calls. Sometimes they come from bars and sometimes from people who are dangerously deranged. So when Steve goes to a strange place for the first time, he does not go alone. Although he was once a wrestler and at another time a bouncer, he asked two friends to go with him. Mike was a reporter for a Long Island newspaper and had been a sprinter in college. George was a former football player who now teaches sociology in high school. Neither believed in ghosts, but they went along for a lark.

It was a cold night, with rain mixed with sleet. As they approached the old Miller place on the muddy road, they could hear a dog howling. "A perfect night for a murder," Mike said, grinning.

There was a sedan parked in front of the house. As they drew up behind it, the doctor at the clinic came out of the front door. He told Steve, "I came because I was worried about the child. Now I'm concerned about the mother, too. The father isn't home. Last night, whatever the dog saw drove him crazy. He's locked up in the barn. I hope you have the answer."

Steve rang the doorbell. A motherly-looking woman answered. She was trying hard to seem calm, but her face was blotched with crying. She welcomed the three young men and invited them to sit down; her husband would be home soon.

When she went to get coffee, Steve followed her out to the kitchen. "Is there anything you haven't told me? I need to know everything."

She set out a tray, avoiding his eyes. "I haven't dared to tell my husband. But I've seen the ghost, too. Twice."

Steve sat down opposite her and waited. Finally she

went on, "As I was coming out of the bathroom last night, before I went to bed, there she was on the landing. The dearest little girl you could hope to see. Long dark hair, like mine, and the most wonderful golden eyes. She put out her arms to me just before she vanished."

"And the second time?"

She blew her nose. "The second time was this morning in the kitchen. I was alone again. She talked to me. She begged me not to send her away. Dr. Kaplan, I don't know what to do!"

"How could it be a choice between a ghost and your own child?"

"You don't understand. Before we adopted Betty, I had a little girl who was born dead. With dark hair."

"You think the ghost is this child?"

She nodded.

Steve put a hand on the woman's arm. "I'll do what I can. You just have to trust me."

Someone had come in the front door. Mrs. Reese hurriedly put cups on the tray and poured the coffee. Steve followed with the cream and sugar. He shook hands with Mr. Reese, who seemed a quiet, respectable man, and asked if he could see Betty alone.

She was a pretty child, but she looked drained and terrified. Her parents had moved the television set into her bedroom and she was staring at it. He sat down in the chair next to her bed and tried to talk to her gently. She didn't answer. She didn't even seem to hear him. When he put a hand on her arm to attract her attention, she flinched and screamed. But she would not look at him.

He asked Mrs. Reese to come upstairs. Together, they

tried to get her out of bed. She submitted, limp and passive. When they tried to get her to stand up, she collapsed in a heap on the floor. Her mother put her back to bed, and Steve went downstairs and said to Mr. Reese, "The first thing you must do is get Betty out of here. She's in danger."

"The doctor talks about a psychiatrist—"

"She doesn't need a psychiatrist. She's not imagining things. Have you any friends you could stay with?"

"Not here. Our family is all in Philadelphia."

"Then you must go to a motel. Can you afford it?"

Mr. Reese nodded. "We can afford it if Betty's in danger. But I'd like to know from what."

Steve said, "You have a vampire in the house."

Mike laughed. A look from Steve shut him up.

Mr. Reese said, "I don't understand. I thought vampires were like bats."

Steve said, "Vampires are ghosts who sap the energy of living creatures so they can borrow their bodies."

"Not that sweet little girl! She couldn't be a vampire!" A cry of agony came from Mrs. Reese.

Steve nodded. "That sweet little girl has been trying to kill your daughter. She almost succeeded. She's no harmless ghost and no child who could be yours. She is evil all through. All I can do is try to get rid of her. I'll come tomorrow at the same time with my friends, if they can."

Mike redeemed himself by calling a motel where he knew the manager and getting a special rate for the Reeses.

After the couple had left, carrying Betty wrapped in blankets, Steve and his two friends went over the house. It was an old place, with thick stone walls. Despite the fact that it was spotless, a tribute to Mrs. Reese's housekeeping, there was an odor that grew stronger as they reached the cellar, where it became sickening.

"I'm getting out," Mike said. "I'll wait for you in the car."

Steve and George went over the house again. Steve studied the footprints on the bedroom wall of the room where the Reeses slept. As he did so, he felt someone staring at him. He turned around. A child with long, black hair was standing in the corner, an expression of hatred on her small face, her lips curled up over too-long yellowing teeth. But most horrible of all were her eyes. They were like burning coals.

They left shortly after that. As they drove away, they heard the miserable dog howling.

Steve said to Mike, "Can you find out why the house is supposed to be haunted? There is usually some reason, even if the rumors come from kids."

Mike said he'd make inquiries at the paper. And George volunteered to find out who owned the house, and talk to them. They agreed to meet on Sunday night at Steve's place.

When Mike came in, he told Steve, "All I could gather is that nobody stays in the house long. There must be a good reason." A few minutes later, George came in. "An old biddy owns the place. She's a widow. Her husband's mother was a Miller. All she can think about is money. The Reeses have gone back to Pennsylvania, but she wouldn't refund the rent they'd paid."

"A nice lady," Steve said sarcastically.

"You can say that again. She's a horror. All she can talk about is how people have cheated her. I had to sit through a long-winded story about how she rented the house cheap to some woman who was bringing over British refugee children during World War II. Apparently she disappeared in the middle of the night, owing rent and leaving the kids without anything to eat."

"The kiddy scandal!" Mike jumped to his feet. "I was in junior high, but everybody was talking about it. She'd punished the children by tying them up and leaving them in the cellar without food or water. One child died."

"A little girl?" Steve asked.

Mike said he'd go back to the office and check. Copies of the newspaper during the war were kept on microfilm in the library. It was after midnight when Steve's phone rang. Mike said, "Right. I found the stories. The girl was nine years old. Her body was found in the cellar. There was a terrible scandal because the child had starved to death. The woman was never caught."

"And the murdered child is still around, looking for a body to invade," said Steve. "I'm going back there tomorrow night. Do you want to come with me?"

George decided to go along, too. So on Monday night, the three men approached the house. The electricity had been shut off, but they had anticipated that and brought flashlights. The doors were locked, but a front window was halfway open and they climbed in the haunted house, feeling like burglars. The smell in the cellar was even stronger than it had been on Friday night. Mike said, "I'm getting out." Suddenly, down the stairs came a huge creature. They turned their flashlights into the face of a snarling dog, with teeth bared. Steve tossed his flashlight into one corner and, while the dog lunged for it, they escaped.

On the way home, they stopped by the police station to report a mad dog at large. The sergeant on the desk looked at them and shook his head. "That old dog has been dead for twenty-four hours. We had to go out yesterday and shoot it. What have you been drinking?"

Around Christmas that year, the Miller place burned to the ground. Nobody was in it, for the stingy woman hadn't been able to find anyone willing to live there. Steve thought that was the end of the story, but about three years later, a pretty young girl walked into his office and called him by name.

"I'm Betty Reese," she said. "I'm visiting in the area and I'd like to see the house where the vampire tried to get me."

Steve told her it had burned down, and a good thing, too. Betty insisted she would like to drive by the ruins. She had her own car outside and Roxanne offered to go with her. She brought along a ouija board. Many psychics use ouija boards to communicate with dead spirits. Letters of the alphabet are arranged on it in a circle. An indicator on the board is moved by the body warmth and psychic powers of the person holding it, spelling out words that are supposed to be messages from the dead.

When they got to the old place, they parked in front of what had been the house. Roxanne said to Betty, "I know I'm psychic and I suspect you are, too. If the girl is still here, I think she might talk to us. You aren't afraid, are you?"

Betty laughed and shook her head. "It all seems funny now, but I must say, it didn't at the time."

As she spoke, a cloud came over the sun, and the day, which had been bright and sunny, grew chilly. Betty shivered. But they went ahead.

Roxanne still has her notes on what the board spelled out. She showed them to me.

The vampire identified herself as "V." She said she'd died in the cellar, where she had been starved and tortured. Asked why she had attacked Betty, she answered, "It's my house. I belong there."

"Even though it has burned down?"

"Yes."

"Why did you try to hurt Betty?"

"Needed her. Needed her. Needed her body."

"Did you hate her?"

"Yes."

"Do you still want her body?"

The ouija board was still. Then they heard a dog howl. Betty's hands shook as she shoved the board away. "That's Blizzard. He howled that way before when he tried to save me. I don't want to stay here anymore. I'm frightened."

She started the car. But when they reached the highway, she stopped the car and looked back. "Poor little kid, it's not her fault she got turned into a vampire. Just the same, I know my parents were right about warning me not to come here. I'm not going to try it again."

About the Author

Isabella Taves has written many short stories and articles for magazines and was once on the staff of *Look* magazine. This is her eleventh book. Among the others were *Not Bad for a Girl,* about a girl who was thrown off the Little League team, and *The Three Lives of Harriet Hubbard Ayer*. She was named for her grandmother, whom you meet in this book.